HALIFAX
MURDERS

MARGARET DRINKALL

First published 2013

The History Press
The Mill, Brimscombe Port
Stroud, Gloucestershire, GL5 2QG
www.thehistorypress.co.uk

British Library Cataloguing in Publication Data.
A catalogue record for this book is available from the British Library.

ISBN 978 0 7524 7949 1

Typesetting and origination by The History Press
Printed in Great Britain

CONTENTS

ACKNOWLEDGEMENTS

Writing a book is not a solitary exercise and it could not be done without the help and encouragement of friends and family. Many thanks, as always, to the skilful editors at The History Press, including Lucy Simpkin for making sense of my ramblings. Grateful thanks go members of my family, particularly to my niece Sue Trickey and her two daughters Genna and Bridie Wanley. I would also like to thank Mr and Mrs Tasker Taylor for their kind permission to take and reproduce pictures of Todmorden Parsonage. I also want to give my thanks to the Friends of Lister Lane Cemetery for permission to use the inscription on the grave of James Edward Jacobs. Lastly, but by no means least, I would like to thank Steve Baxter for helping me with the photographs of Halifax and for bearing patiently and with great stoicism as I reminisced endlessly about the places I knew as a girl.

INTRODUCTION

For many centuries, Halifax was at the centre of the woollen trade, and by the Victorian era was a hub of commercial and industrial activity. Pride of place is given to Piece Hall, which stands in the town centre and was built in 1779. This Grade I listed Georgian masterpiece is unique as the only remaining Cloth Hall in England, where, traditionally, lengths or pieces of cloth were bought and sold.

The introduction of the power loom in the 1820s saw a reduction in the number of handloomers throughout the area, many of whom had previously seen themselves as craftsmen and artisans. By 1839, however, weaving was undertaken in the large factories which were being increasingly built around the town. Many of the former handloom weavers were forced to find other trades to earn a living; even farmers were being forced to work other trades, some becoming slaughter men. Industrialisation had brought an influx of labour into the area and with it poverty and overcrowding, which resulted, inevitably, in a rise in crime.

View of Halifax.

Halifax Piece Hall.

The town is dominated by Beacon Hill, which has its own history of executions. On Saturday, 6 August 1769, Robert Thomas and Matthew Normanton were executed at York for the murder of an exciseman. After the hangings their bodies were returned to Halifax under a heavy guard. The bodies were hung in chains on Beacon Hill, left there as an example to other murderers, and their hands were placed pointing towards the scene of the murder.

People who committed murder in Halifax between 1541 and 1650 would most likely have been beheaded on the gibbet, situated on the aptly named Gibbet Street.

A modern reproduction of the Halifax Gibbet upon the original base.

The condemned cell at York Castle, where prisoners waited for their execution.

The first felon to meet his end in this fashion was a man named Richard Bentley, or Beverley, although there is no record as to what his crime was. The last to be executed by this method was Anthony Mitchell of Sowerby, on 30 April 1650. By the Victorian period, the punishment for committing murder was handled in a very different way. Anyone charged with committing murder in Halifax would be tried at the local Magistrates' Court and if found guilty were sent to stand trial at the assizes in York or Leeds. If they were found guilty again they would be hanged on the scaffold outside the castle at York, or Armley Gaol in Leeds. These were usually public executions which attracted thousands of people eager to see the committed hanged. In the 1860s, public execution was abolished in favour of private execution; now, instead of the felon's death being a spectacle, it was announced by a black flag being raised into the air from within the walls of the gaol or castle, indicating that the law had been carried out to the letter.

Margaret Drinkall, 2013

MURDERED BY HIS FATHER

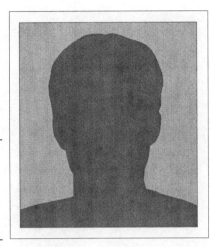

Suspect:	Eli Lumb
Age:	Forty-four
Charge:	Murder
Sentence:	Discharged

In September 1839, the people of Halifax heard of the atrocious murder of a son by his father. The murderer was a man named Eli Lumb, aged forty-four, who traded in multiple things including weaving, butchery and farriery. He lived with his wife and seven children – four sons and three daughters – in an overcrowded cottage. The cottage was made up of four rooms with two on the ground floor, one of which was used as a weaving shed and held two looms, and the other as a kitchen. Upstairs there were two bedrooms. The first bedroom contained two double beds, one shared by the oldest son Thomas, aged thirty, and his brother Joseph, aged twenty-three, and in the other bed was John, aged sixteen, and Eli junior, aged ten. Eli senior and his wife occupied the second bedroom, whilst in a corner, under a bundle of clothes, slept thirteen-year-old Elizabeth. Lumb's eldest daughter was married and lived next door in another cottage which was attached to the same building as her parents' house. Thomas was expecting to leave the family home following his marriage to a local girl. It was reported that Lumb became increasingly addicted to alcohol. Unfortunately, this combination of drunkenness and overcrowding led to many incidents of domestic abuse against his long-suffering wife and children.

On Thursday 19 September, Lumb was due to butcher a cow belonging to Mr Thomas Hitchen of Ripponden Wood. In the afternoon he set off to Ripponden Wood, only to find upon his arrival that the cow had died and been taken away to the knacker's yard. No doubt furious about this

St Peter's Church, Sowerby.

unexpected loss of income, he called in at the New Shop, a public house owned by James Heaps in the little township of Sowerby.

Later in the day he was joined by his son Joseph, who spent some time drinking with his father. About 7 p.m. Joseph told his father that he was going home, to which his father replied, 'I'll be along in a short while'. Just before 9 p.m. his wife, who was standing in the lane leading to their cottage, heard him coming towards her shouting and making a great noise. She castigated her husband for causing such a fuss and he told her to 'hold her tongue'. Once inside, Mrs Lumb continued to berate her husband and he threatened that if she did not desist he would run away and leave her. After further altercations the irate Lumb punched his wife several times and then pushed her towards the front door. Before she could protest, he bundled his wife out of the house and locked the door. Pocketing the key he went upstairs to bed, leaving her in the garden. Normally he would leave the leather pouch containing his three butchering knives downstairs in the kitchen. This time, however, he took the knives upstairs with him. Blowing out the candle, Lumb got undressed and climbed into bed.

Thomas, hearing his mother shouting outside, went downstairs to let her back in but when he reached the front door he found the key missing, so he went to retrieve it from his father. By this point, Lumb – who had been woken up – was infuriated with his son, who he now accused of taking his wife's side; he threatened that if Thomas let his mother back into the house he would 'stick him'. The two men started to scuffle in the darkened bedroom. Upon hearing the noise, the other children woke up and ran to the bedroom, where they witnessed the sight of their father struggling and punching their oldest brother. They ran to the bottom of the stairs, in fright, where they could hear their mother pounding on the door. It was at this point that Lumb drew out one of the knives from the pouch at the side of the bed and lunged at his son, stabbing him in the thigh. Holding his leg, Thomas made his way downstairs and got a fire iron from the kitchen, which he carried back up the stairs. He hit his father twice across the head before Lumb, now incredibly angry, attacked his son once more, delivering three more stab wounds – two to his side and one fatal wound to his left breast, burying the knife to the hilt. By this time it was half past ten in the evening, and the younger son, John, managed to get the key out of his father's pocket and let his mother in. The two younger children – Eli junior and Elizabeth – ran next door to the safety of their sister's house, whilst Joseph, John and their mother went to tend to Thomas' wounds.

'lunged at his son, stabbing him in the thigh'

Lumb could now see the state of his eldest son's health and he gathered him into his arms, crying out, 'Oh Tom, speak to me, cannot thou speak to me?' The father, mother and two sons looked upon the scene in the bedroom with horror; the silence only broken by Thomas's last sobs as he died. When he realised that his son was dead, Lumb hastily donned his outdoor clothes and ran downstairs, crying out, 'I shall be hanged for this'. Lumb's other son, Joseph, followed him and tried to hold on to him, but he dashed out of the house and up the lane.

A constable was called to the house and, after listening to Mrs Lumb and her sons, ordered that the surrounding fields and sheds be searched. By now, other neighbours had gathered, having heard the commotion, and joined in with the search. Within a short distance of the house the two remaining knives were found and the constable tracked Lumb's footprints towards a nearby dam. The constable thought that Lumb was going to drown himself but was astonished to see that the footprints carried on past the dam, heading in the direction of a place known locally as Cobs Castle. The search for Eli Lumb continued and he was finally found in Bradford two days later and brought back to Halifax, where he was arrested for the wilful murder of his son.

On Saturday 21 September an inquest was held at the Sportsman Inn, Halifax, before the coroner Thomas Lee Esq. Prior to the inquest, as was customary at the time, the jury were taken to the house where the dead man lay in order to view the body. A reporter, who accompanied the jury, stated that:

> The body provided a dreadful spectacle. The deceased man had a wound in his right thigh; his hand had also been stabbed, as was the right breast. But it was the wound in the left breast which had killed him. The dead man was shirtless although the blood-soaked shirt lay on the floor of the bedroom.

One of the jurors picked up the shirt and noted that the cuts and blood on the shirt corresponded with the cuts on the body. It was reported that the bedroom was in a terrible state, with blood and gore stains splashed all over the walls and floorboards. Lumb, who had been captured that morning and was now in custody, attended the inquest and wept bitterly throughout the proceedings. Mrs Lumb told the coroner about her life with her husband, admitting that he was not the soberest of men. The coroner asked her about Lumb's relationship with his sons and she told him that they argued from time to time, but he had always got on well with all of them, in particular Thomas.

Lumb's neighbours gave their own detailed descriptions of the altercation and how they had joined in the search that night. A female neighbour told the coroner and the jury that Thomas was a sober and hard-working young man, who had been employed as a weaver at Makin Place, Soyland, and had the respect and good opinion of all who knew him. The next to give evidence was Joseph, who stated that while in the public house, he and his father had about four pints each. Joseph left around seven o'clock and tried to get his father to come with him but was unsuccessful; his father remained in the pub drinking with his friends. He said that when he got home, he told his mother that Lumb had stayed on and she began to fret.

Mr Bland, the surgeon who examined Thomas's body at the house, described the wounds that he had found. He said that three were slight, only one of them going into the cartilage of one of the ribs, cutting it in half. However, it was the fourth stab wound which has been the cause of death. The surgeon told the jury that he had completed the post-mortem the following day and had found the fatal wound to be two inches long. The knife had gone through the chest and straight into the heart, causing an almost instant death. Lumb told the coroner, 'I cannot remember anything except him striking me with the fire iron. I was dizzy for a long time, I cannot tell how long.' The jury took very little time in finding Lumb guilty of wilful murder and he was sent to the spring assizes to stand trial.

On Thursday, 11 March 1840, Lumb appeared before Mr Justice Erskine and the jury found that there was no true bill to answer. It was common practice before each assizes started for the jury to examine every bill of indictment for each prisoner. If it was felt that the prisoner was not guilty, there was not enough evidence or there were other mitigating circumstances, the action would be dropped and no true bill found. In this case, Mr Knowles, for the prosecution, rose and stated that no evidence would be offered and the jury, by the direction of Mr Justice Erskine, found a verdict of acquittal in favour of the prisoner, which allowed Lumb to be discharged.

CASE TWO   1865

'OH MOTHER, DON'T POISON ME'

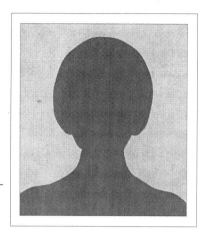

Suspect:	Leah Atkinson
Age:	Unknown
Charge:	Murder
Sentence:	Discharged

During the Victorian period, having a child out of wedlock was most definitely frowned upon. It was usually deemed to be the woman's fault for allowing herself to be seduced by a man; little blame was attached to the putative father of the child, resulting in both the mother and child usually being shunned by 'respectable' society.

Portland Road, Halifax.

Leah Atkinson lived with her daughter, Betty, on Portland Road, Range Bank, Halifax, in a lodging house kept by Martha Booth. On 12 June 1856, Leah and a neighbour, Elizabeth Holgate, went to the market place in town to collect some laudanum for Betty, who was ill and had been steadily getting worse. Entering the druggists owned by Mr Wood, she asked the boy who served in the shop for a pennyworth of laudanum. He said that he was not authorised to serve this to her, as it was poison. He called for his master, Mr Wood, who came into the shop from the back room. He asked Atkinson how old her daughter was and she replied that she was almost twelve. He stated that he would give her some laudanum, providing she gave her daughter no more than ten drops. Atkinson promised that she would not, so Mr Woods gave her the medicine in a bottle clearly marked 'laudanum poison'.

On her return to the lodging house, Atkinson found Betty in the kitchen, along with some of the other lodgers; one of whom, Emma Heywood, took the bottle from her and stated that it read 'poison' on the label. Atkinson, who was unable to read, went to give her daughter some of the laudanum in a cup of tea. Betty was clearly unhappy and said to her mother, 'Oh mother, don't poison me,' and her mother replied, 'Thou fool, thou's no occasion to be frightened of me poisoning thee, I like thee too well for that.' Fellow lodger Emma Heywood, in order to reassure the little girl, took a spoonful herself but, despite all of her assurances, Betty died the next morning.

Mr Laurence Bramley, the surgeon who had been treating Betty for a disease of the lungs, was called; he saw the body and signed the death certificate. Suspicions surrounding the death of the child, however, would not go away and it was not long before they were brought to the attention of the Halifax police force. Atkinson, after being interviewed by the police, was arrested and charged with poisoning her daughter with laudanum. The coroner was informed and the decision to exhume the child's body was approved. The coroner also instructed surgeon Mr Bramley to conduct a post-mortem on the body.

An inquest was held before coroner Mr George Dyson Esq. on Friday 20 June at 3.30 p.m. at the Bay Horse Inn. The jury was selected and a local manufacturer, Mr John Foster Esq., was elected to act as foreman. The first witness called forward was Elizabeth Holgate, who had accompanied Atkinson to Halifax for the laudanum. She talked about the exchange in the chemists shop and stated that she had seen Atkinson give the drops to Betty, but said that she did not see exactly how many she had put into the tea. Mrs Holgate was asked about Atkinson's relationship with her daughter and said that Leah had spoken very disparaging about Betty on several occasions. She claimed that Atkinson had told her, 'If the child does not die, I will give her some stuff to make it so.' The coroner asked her what her own relations with Atkinson were and Holgate told him that Atkinson had confronted her about all the lies she claimed Holgate had told the neighbours just that week.

'If the child does not die, I will give her some stuff to make it so'

Emma Heywood then gave evidence and said that she had lodged at the house for about two months and that she had always seen Atkinson deal with the child in a kind manner. She told the jury that Betty had been ill for all of the time that she had lodged at the house, and it was generally known that Betty had problems with her chest and had not been expected to live for much longer. She proceeded to tell them about the night that Atkinson had brought home the bottle and how the child had reacted when she had read out the label. Witnesses assembled in the courtroom heard how she had tried to reassure the child by consuming about half a teaspoon of laudanum, roughly the same quantity that she saw Atkinson give to her daughter. However, she claimed that the liquid was given on a teaspoon and not in tea as the previous witness had testified. Elizabeth Holgate was recalled and stated that although Emma Heywood had taken the laudanum by teaspoon, Atkinson gave Betty the laudanum in a cup of tea, which she particularly remembered seeing on the table.

Mr Benjamin Wood, the druggist of Northgate, stated that he remembered the prisoner coming into his shop and asking for the pennyworth of laudanum, which was approximately two drachms (approximately 120 drops). He described how he had labelled the bottle 'Poison', and he brought a similar one with him to the inquest for the jury to see. He told them that after he had enquired what she needed the laudanum for, he instructed Atkinson to give her daughter just five drops, and not to exceed ten drops. He stated that when he had examined the remainder of the laudanum which was left in the bottle, he discovered that, out of the 120 drops issued, 30 drops had been used.

Atkinson then gave her evidence and sobbed bitterly throughout. She told the court that a friend had recommended giving the drops to Betty and that when she got home she intended throwing the bottle away. However, her landlady, Martha Booth, had urged her not to throw it away and to give the child some in order to ease her breathing and the constant pain in her chest. Sobbing, she told the coroner that she had always done her best for the child and had starved herself to make sure that Betty had all the medicine she needed.

Mr Lawrence Bramley, the surgeon, was called and was asked to give his opinion on how much laudanum Betty would have ingested. He informed the court that, allowing for the amount taken by Emma Heywood, he judged it to have been around 15 drops. He also reported the results of the post-mortem, which had revealed that Betty had been very emaciated, but there was little sign of decomposition. There were signs of recent inflammation of the lower bowels, as well as signs of older inflammation. The stomach contained about an ounce of what he described as gritty fluid, but apart from that the stomach was very healthy. There was extensive disease of the right lung and he had no doubt that the child had died from an effusion on the chest. He also told the coroner that, in his opinion, he had been surprised that Betty had lived as long as she had and that the laudanum could have had no effect on the cause of death. The coroner thanked Mr Bramley for the clarity of his account before he proceeded to tell the jury that they needed to keep this in consideration when deciding their verdict. Without leaving the room the jury returned a verdict of death by natural causes.

It seems, in this instance, that this case was the result of a gossiping neighbour, Elizabeth Holgate, who seemed determined to vilify Leah Atkinson. Her supposed comments about wanting to be rid of Betty were not corroborated by other lodgers in the house, who had clearly stated that the child had been ill for a long time. Modern medicine now finds it astonishing that laudanum was acceptable as a soothing medicine in the Victorian era, but it was widely given to even the youngest of children; it was used extensively during teething to enable the child to have a good nights' sleep. The inaccuracy of measuring the drug was also an issue: what is an acceptable drop to a chemist might not be the same for a mother of a distressed child.

CASE THREE   1857

'I CAME TO MURDER HIM AND I HAVE DONE IT'

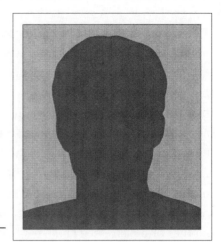

Suspect: John Ackroyd
Age: Unknown
Charge: Murder
Sentence: Penal Servitude

In 1857, a shoemaker named John Ackroyd went to live at the house of Jonathon Houldsworth, a fellow shoemaker, following the breakdown of his marriage. Houldsworth, aged seventy-one, was in receipt of parish relief and took in lodgers at his house in Trafalgar, near Halifax, to make a little extra money. When Ackroyd took up lodgings with Houldsworth, he was informed that Houldsworth would be shortly giving the house up and moving elsewhere, but that he could lodge there until he moved out. Ackroyd had difficulty finding somewhere else to live and as a consequence remained in the house for some weeks once the old man had moved. Meanwhile, Houldsworth took the tenancy of another house and found himself a lodger by the name of Mrs Ann Thomas.

Once Ackroyd had moved out, Houldsworth returned to the house in Trafalgar, only to find that Ackroyd had taken some of the smaller items of furniture with him to his new lodgings. Houldsworth challenged him, claiming that he had no right to take furniture that did not belong to him. Even when Ackroyd moved to more new lodgings the two men continued to argue. Matters became worse when Ackroyd heard that Houldsworth was making sexual remarks about his wife. He claimed to have heard Houldsworth saying that his wife wanted to sleep with him.

The argument between the two men came to a head on Friday, 17 July 1857 after Ackroyd had been drinking in a public house at King Cross. A man named Simpson started up a conversation with him and noted that Ackroyd was already quite drunk by 6.30 p.m. Ackroyd told him the story Houldsworth had been spreading about his wife and he became very angry, shouting about what he would do to him when he next saw him. Simpson told Ackroyd to calm down and to not entertain such foolish notions about revenge. That was when Ackroyd declared he would cut off Houldsworth's head that very night before he went to sleep. After trying unsuccessfully to placate him, Simpson recalled Ackroyd telling him, 'The next time you see me it will be at York Castle, where I shall be hanged.'

Ackroyd went back to his lodgings, where he picked up two sharp knives; he then went to Houldsworth lodgings, arriving there about 9.30 p.m., and told the lodger, Mrs Thomas, that he 'wished to speak to the old man'. Houldsworth, who was eating his supper by the fire, shouted through, 'Take yourself off John Ackroyd; I have nothing at all to say to you.' Without speaking, Ackroyd rushed up to Houldsworth, drew out one of the knives and made a slash at his throat, inflicting a dreadful wound. Houldsworth did not see it coming as he had his back to his

York Castle – site of the gallows.

attacker. Ackroyd then stabbed him on the cheek and, with his left hand, grasped the old man by the throat in order to slash it again. Mrs Thomas bravely seized Ackroyd and tried to pull him away; but he still kept hold of Houldsworth. Ackroyd continued to try to drag the old man out of his chair and succeeded in drawing the sharp knife across his victim's throat. Mrs Thomas continued to struggle with Ackroyd and, seeing the blood coming from Houldsworth's throat, she screamed out 'Murder!' At this point, several neighbours arrived and broke up the struggle. Before leaving the house Ackroyd addressed the crowd, which had begun to assemble outside, stating: 'I have come to do it and I have done it.'

'Seeing the blood coming from Houldsworth's throat, she screamed out "Murder!"'

Two surgeons were called to attend to the injured man, who had two very serious cuts across his throat. Indeed, the wounds were considered so bad that the surgeons stayed with Houldsworth for the whole night. On Saturday morning, Ackroyd was arrested and taken before the Halifax magistrates, charged with cutting and stabbing with the intent to kill Houldsworth. The magistrate, Mr G.B. Browne, thought that given the precarious state Houldsworth's life was in, it would be advisable to take his dying deposition and, accompanied by his clerk, the whole of the jury and the prisoner, he went to Houldsworth's house for that purpose. But one of the surgeons attending the injured man said that he had suffered so much from the wounds that they could not allow him to speak. That afternoon, Houldsworth rallied a little and made a statement to the magistrate, in which he said:

I am seventy one years of age and live at this house. Last night at 9.30 p.m. the prisoner came and asked to see me. I was sat downstairs and was quite well when he came in. He came across the floor towards me and seized me by the throat with his left hand. I did not see then that he had a knife but he drew something across my face and cut me. Ann Thomas seized him and tried to pull him away; he still kept hold of me and tried to drag me out.

When asked if he had anything he wished to ask Houldsworth, Ackroyd said he wanted to know why he had circulated such scandal about his wife. Houldsworth replied, 'I never said any scandal about her.' The deposition was then signed and Ackroyd returned back to the Magistrates' Court and he was remanded until the following week.

On Friday 24 July it was reported that Houldsworth's condition was getting better. The following day, at noon, Ackroyd was once again taken before the magistrates. Superintendent Pearson started the case, stating that Ackroyd was a married man but that some time ago, as a consequence of some trouble at home, he had gone to lodge with Houldsworth. He said that Houldsworth had moved into new lodgings, which sparked the argument about the missing furniture – his new lodger, Mrs Thomas, was in need of certain items which Ackroyd had taken, so Houldsworth went to his house demanding that he return the property. Pearson told the court that Ackroyd, at this point, started to abuse the old man and threatened

King Cross, where Ackroyd had his last drink.

to kill him. Pearson then continued to say that while in the prison cell, Ackroyd had confessed to a fellow prisoner that he had gone into the pub at King Cross to purchase a glass or two of rum to give him the courage to carry out his task. He had also confessed to going to Houldsworth's house with the clear intention of stabbing him. Ackroyd told the other prisoner that he had intended to make the attack so sudden that none of the lodgers would be able to interfere and stop him.

One of the surgeons, Mr W. Nowell, praised Mrs Thomas for her quick action, without which, he told the court, Houldsworth would have died very quickly as his wounds were so deep. He described them, stating that, 'One cut was exactly across the throat and almost three inches long and a quarter of an inch deep. The other commenced at the right side of the mouth extending beneath the chin and severed all the structures down to the lower jawbone.' He then told the magistrate that, 'There were four serious arteries severed; two in each wound required ligatures. By the time I reached the house, Houldsworth had lost at least a quart of blood. The windpipe was slashed, but thankfully not severed.'

Halifax Magistrates' Court, where Ackroyd was tried.

The jury found Ackroyd guilty and the prisoner, who appeared to be very calm and collected, stated that he would reserve his defence. He was committed to York Castle for trial at the next assizes. The local newspaper reported that, 'Since Ackroyd has been in custody, the prisoner has said to other prisoners that he wished he had used his other, sharper knife, as he should then have succeeded in cutting Houldsworth's head off.' As to the outcome of the trial, the same newspaper reported that, 'He appears very careless of the outcome, remarking only that he wishes to die.'

On Saturday 5 December, Ackroyd was brought before the assize judge, Mr Justice Williams. Mr Blanchard and Mr Gresham were for the prosecution and Mr Price defended the prisoner. The witness, Simpson, took the stand and told the court about his conversation with Ackroyd in the pub at King Cross. He described him as being very excited and appeared to be drunk, but gave the opinion that Ackroyd seemed to know perfectly well what he was doing. Mrs Thomas then spoke about the night of the attack, explaining how, as Ackroyd lunged at Houldsworth for the second time, she struck the hand which held the knife but was unable to prevent him slashing it across Houldsworth's throat.

Ackroyd's defence stated that he admitted he had purposely gone to the house with the intention of hurting Houldsworth, but that he had no intention to murder him. Mr Price then asked the jury to acquit him of the more serious charge and substitute the lesser charge of inflicting bodily harm. However, the prosecution told the jury that Ackroyd had clearly made a statement about his intentions, not only to the crowd gathered at Houldsworth's house, but also repeated it to the arresting sergeant. The sergeant recorded in his notes that Ackroyd had said, 'I went

'I went on purpose to kill him and I hope that he will be dead before morning'

on purpose to kill him and I hope that he will be dead before morning.' No doubt in an attempt to rectify this, the defence presented a witness

who gave Ackroyd an excellent character, stating that he was a quiet and
peaceable man for most of the
time. However, because of his
statements to various witnesses about his intention
to kill Houldsworth, the
jury had no option but to
find Ackroyd guilty. When
asked if he had anything
to say against this judgement, Ackroyd replied that
he hoped his Lordship would
have mercy on him as in his
sober moments, he did not
intend to murder Houldsworth.
The judge contradicted him,
saying that there was no reason-
able doubt that he fully intended to
murder the old man and for that
crime his life was forfeited to the
law. He then placed the black cap
on his head and sentenced him to death.

Judge with black cap.

On 15 January 1858, it was recorded that the Secretary of State had
intervened and directed that Ackroyd's death sentence be reduced to fifteen
years' penal servitude.

CASE FOUR 1858

MURDER IN A NEWSPAPER OFFICE

Suspect:	William Blackburn Dawson
Age:	Twenty
Charge:	Murder
Sentence:	Penal Servitude

In 1832, the *Halifax Guardian* made its debut as a weekly newspaper informing the people of Halifax about events which were happening both locally and nationally.

On Wednesday, 5 May 1858 the newspaper offices were crowded with people. There was a lull during the lunchtime hours, but by 2 p.m. many of the workers had returned to work. Some of them went into the news office on the second floor, which overlooked George Street, whilst others went through the news office and into the jobbing room behind it. In the middle of the jobbing room were two press frames, placed back-to-back. James Edward Jacobs, aged thirty-four, worked at one and at the other was an apprentice named William Blackburn Dawson, a youth aged about twenty, who had worked at the *Halifax Guardian* for six years.

Dawson went into the news office and asked the other workers if any of them had some snuff for Jacobs. After he had been given a box, he returned to the jobbing room. No words were exchanged between the men, and Dawson picked up one of the dumbbells in the office – owned by another apprentice named John Crosley – and started to exercise with it. As the dumbbells were regularly used by the men, no one thought anything of it. Suddenly, and without any provocation, Dawson began to beat Jacobs over the head with the dumbbell, knocking him to the ground. Dawson then grabbed an axe that had been placed near the

Advertisement for the *Halifax Guardian*.

fireplace and hit Jacobs over the head, felling the poor man forward onto the press. Then, emitting an unnerving shriek, he continued to club Jacobs over the head with the axe. Three other men working in the room went to interrupt the attack but Dawson turned on them, once again emitting a fearful shriek. He drove them out of the jobbing room and into the news office before locking the door behind them and continuing his attack on the, by now, dead man. Men from the news office desperately tried to break the door down, as they could hear what could only be described as a desperate beating noise as Dawson continued making the high-pitched shriek. Peering through a gap in the door, they saw Dawson take up a press pin – a piece of metal which was five or six feet in length – from the machine and continue to attack his dead victim. Two men named Bates and Tiffany began beating the door, trying to break it down. When it finally gave way they found Jacobs body on the floor and Dawson standing nearby; a bloody press pin in his hand. He attempted to escape, but was prevented by the men who were now crowding into the jobbing room.

Jacobs body was lying face up, surrounded by a pool of blood with brains and other matter splattered across the floor and walls. The deceased man had been powerfully built and in a proper fight, it was said, he could defend himself well, but with the speed with which Dawson had hit him he had not stood a chance. The fatal injuries were confined to the front part of the head and both legs had been attacked; the wounds penetrating down to the bone.

Dawson appeared somewhat wild and savage looking, and his shirt sleeves and trousers were covered with splattered blood and brains from the dead man. The police were called and Dawson was arrested and taken to the police station. Upon his arrest, he told them that he hadn't finished the job as he had wanted to cut Jacobs head off and throw it into George Street.

'A pool of blood with brains and other matter splattered across the floor and walls'

Police enquiries showed that Dawson was still serving as an apprentice under the tutelage of the proprietor of the newspaper, Mr Walker. His colleagues described him as a quiet young man who had never shown any animosity towards Jacobs; they even took lunch together on several occasions. No one who worked at the *Guardian* offices had noted anything concerning in Dawson's behaviour prior to the attack.

At the police station, whilst giving his statement, it was said that Dawson appeared to be not exactly excited but that he had a 'wildness in his eye'. He could give no reason for the attack and it was generally thought that he had been suddenly possessed with a violent rage when he attacked the older man. Yet despite this common belief, the attack had been premeditated. The errand lad for the newspaper offices told the police that he had left the axe in the coal place downstairs, where it was used to chop up wood. Before lunch, Dawson had taken it to the jobbing room, as if in readiness for the attack.

The inquest into the murder was held at the White Lion Hotel by the coroner, Mr Dyson, at 7 p.m. on the day of the murder. A solicitor attended on behalf of Mr Walker, and another solicitor, Mr Franklin, appeared on behalf of Dawson. The coroner asked that the inquest be adjourned, as little could be achieved that evening. Mr Franklin stated that as the events had happened so quickly, he had only had the briefest time to speak with his client. He stated that he was anxious to know more about the character and conduct of his client before the examination of witnesses could take place. The jury then proceeded to the *Halifax Guardian* offices, where they viewed the body; the inquest was adjourned to the following day.

When the inquest resumed, Dawson was in attendance surrounded by some of the largest policemen on the squad. Great curiosity had been aroused because of the nature of the crime and crowds were expected to attend. One of the compositors, James Hislop, spoke of Dawson as being a quiet genial lad who always did everything he was told and never lost his temper, but that during the attack he appeared to be excited and in a frenzy, as he threatened anyone who came near him that he would 'kill them all'. Mr Tucker, the surgeon, gave evidence as to the state of the prisoner's health. He said that Dawson had been weak-minded from his childhood and that some years ago he had gone to consult him about an imaginary infirmity of a most peculiar nature. On hearing this, the prisoner rushed to attack Mr Tucker, almost screaming in fury, and it took ten men to hold him down. So great was his fury that the coroner and the jury had to adjourn to another room so that Mr Tucker could continue. He stated that:

> After this consultation, Dawson came back two days later still convinced that he was ill. He then returned every day for three successive days and would not believe that there was nothing wrong with him. I had absolutely no doubt of Dawson's insanity and would not have been surprised to hear that he had committed suicide. However, I thought him too meek and mild to ever kill someone.

Nevertheless, his doubt had resulted in him warning several people about Dawson. He stated that in his opinion Dawson was undoubtedly insane when he committed this act. Once he had completed the post-mortem on the dead man he relayed that he had found over twenty-five separate injuries, which had been inflicted while Jacobs had been on the floor. He said the first blow would have caused instant death, as it drove the skull into the brain.

The jury only retired for five minutes before returning with a guilty verdict and Dawson was ordered to take his trial at the next assizes. Before he was removed to York, Dawson was permitted to speak with his parents and Mr Tucker, the surgeon. He apologised to the doctor for his behaviour, but complained of pains in his head which had not allowed him to sleep for some time.

On Friday morning he was taken to Halifax train station, where he was conveyed to York on the 6.14 train, in the custody of Inspector Gawkroger and PC Turner. When he arrived at the station, despite the early hour, there were hundreds of people assembled to see him take his departure. He appeared calm and collected as he took his seat, hand-cuffed to the officers in the railway carriage. When he arrived at York it seems that his notoriety had spread, the crowd of people so great that he had to spend half an hour at the Station Hotel until enough of the crowd could be dispersed, allowing him to continue his journey to the castle. Upon arrival, he was interviewed by the prison surgeon, Mr Anderson, which was usual practice for new prisoners. The surgeon found that even when asked the most innocuous questions, Dawson would assume a fighting position, shouting at him that he had no right to ask him such questions, and he would have to be restrained.

On Saturday 8 May, the body of James Edward Jacobs was interred at Halifax Cemetery. So popular a figure had he been in the town that hundreds of people gathered in the cemetery grounds whilst the burial took place. The headstone to his grave reads: 'In memory of James Edward Jacobs of Halifax, who died 5th May 1858, aged 34 years. "Watch and pray for ye know not when the hour cometh".'

It was reported that while he was incarcerated awaiting trial, Dawson had been quite lucid, although when questioned he was reluctant to refer to the murder. His only outburst had been on one occasion in the chapel, where he began to act so violently that divine service was disturbed and he had to be removed. His parents visited him before the trial and to them he showed the greatest reluctance to talk about the murder.

On Wednesday 14 July, William Dawson was brought before the judge, Mr Baron Martin, at the York assizes. Mr Shaw, for the prosecution, opened the case and gave an account of the murder of Jacobs. For the defence, Mr Price stated that the prisoner could give no reason for the attack and there was no motive as to why Dawson should have murdered the deceased man. James Hislop told the judge that he had worked at the newspaper for six years and had been one of the men in the room with Dawson when he began his attack. He stated that his attention was drawn to the events by someone saying that Dawson was killing Jacobs.

Halifax railway station, where Dawson was conveyed to York under police guard.

He described Dawson as being of a close disposition and of very studious habits, and that he frequently sat for hours, gazing vacantly whilst at work. But the one person he seemed to be closest to was Jacobs. Another man who was present at the time of the attack, Samuel Harris, corroborated Hişlop's evidence and admitted to being petrified by the manner and appearance of Dawson. Harris had noted that his emotional state seemed to have changed in the last month before the murder. The next witness was Dr Turner, who had known Dawson from childhood. He told the court that, in his opinion, Dawson suffered from a form of monomania – once he had struck the first blow it prevented him from having any self-control. The defence agreed and Mr Price stated that:

> He did not intend to dispute the facts and the question for the jury was simple: would they consign an unfortunate man to the gallows, or save his life. That could only be resolved by them, and they alone had to decide whether, at the time of the murder, Dawson was aware of his

The grave of James Edward Jacobs at Halifax Cemetery.

actions. If the jury thought that at the time the prisoner was suffering from insanity, they must acquit him on those grounds. Indeed, the manner of Jacob's death could only be described as the act of a madman.

At this stage of the proceedings, the prosecution stated that they would withdraw, and the judge directed the jury to acquit the prisoner on the grounds of insanity – he was ordered to be kept at Her Majesty's pleasure. Throughout the trial Dawson had looked decidedly vacant, proving the judgement to be a sound one. He was safely guarded and watched by two officers of the prison, who stood on either side of him.

Cases like these are very shocking to the people who witness them, particularly when the murderer has shown little aggression beforehand. Mental health was poorly understood in the nineteenth century, and the cases that had been diagnosed were listed as religious mania, melancholia and delirium tremens. Little idea about how to treat such illnesses was known, or understood, and many bewildered medical men resorted, in desperation, to leeching. Depression in women was not acknowledged in the Victorian era and post-natal depression was unheard of, as seen in the following case.

CASE FIVE 1864

'I'VE DONE IT AND WHAT'S DONE CAN'T BE UNDONE'

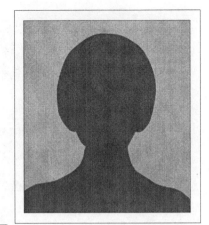

Suspect: Mary Dyson
Age: Unknown
Charge: Murder
Sentence: Penal Servitude

West Riding towns like Halifax were a magnet to immigrants coming from other countries, hoping to find work. In the nineteenth century, so many Irish people came to the town that it had its own Irish Quarter. Despite the promise of better wages and working conditions, the impact of being in another country, often without the comfort of parents and relatives to support them, had a large impact on family life. For many it was just too much to take.

Mary and William Dyson were married in 1859 in Sligo, Ireland. William had been discharged from the army and was working as a stone-mason and lodging with Mary's parents at Sligo, which is where they first met – they were married a few months later. Soon after the marriage they returned to England, but it was hard for William to find work and they had to return to Ireland in November 1862, to live with Mary's parents once again. Determined to find work, William travelled back to England without his family and found employment at Lowertown, Rastrick, near Halifax. When Mary rejoined her husband they lodged at the house of Mr and Mrs Aspinall, but they had been looking for a house of their own.

On Monday, 11 April 1864 the couple and their two children, Mary, aged two-and-a-half years, and Archibald, aged five months, moved to another cottage on Ogden Lane, Rastrick. The new house was much bigger, although the couple had little in the way of furniture or belongings. Mary often told her husband that she was depressed and that she didn't know what to do with herself during the day while he was at work. William was concerned about her, as her conduct led him to believe that she was not always in her right mind – she herself had told him that her mind was uneasy. The previous winter he had been out of work once again and having little food and money may have contributed to the decline in her state of mind.

On Wednesday 13 April, William got up to go to work at Brookfoot, which was about two miles away from his home. Mary woke up before him and, as usual, made his breakfast. William left the house at about 6.20 a.m. and when he left, Mary was in the kitchen and the children were still in bed. At 7.15 p.m. he went to see his aunt in Ellend Edge to buy some utensils from her, before returning home at around 9 p.m. He noted that Mary seemed to be rather quiet and a little downcast. In order to try to alleviate her depression, the couple discussed whether Mary and the children should go back and live with her parents in Ireland for a short while, for a break. But after discussing it, they both knew that they couldn't afford the fare, which Mary seemed to accept. They went to bed at about 12.30 a.m. and William was up again at 6 a.m. Once again, Mary prepared breakfast for him and she walked with him to the door. She had spoken very little that morning, but gave him no reason to seriously worry about her state of mind.

Later that morning, Mary appeared at the house of a neighbour named Mary Walker to ask her to mangle some clothes for her. Mrs Walker had not met Mary before but she later commented that she seemed very friendly. Mary left the clothes to be mangled before returning to her own house.

At around 9.20 a.m., Mary appeared at PC Bracewell's house (he was one of the West Riding constabulary stationed at Rastrick) and told him that she had killed her two children. She told PC Bracewell:

I have murdered my two children, these hands have done it; if I have millions of pounds in the world I would give them all to recall the deed that I have done. William has been a good husband and an affectionate father, and I have deprived him of both titles. I gave Mary a bit of bread and then killed her, wretch that I am.

Leaving Mary at his house in the charge of his wife, PC Bracewell called for the other village constable, PC William Ambler, and they both went to Mary's house. There they found the door open and the bodies of the two children, which appeared to have been placed very carefully at either side of the kitchen table. In the little girl's hand was a piece of bread, which she had been eating when she was killed. There was a good deal of blood, and five or six inches behind the youngest child they found an open razor – blood still evident on the blade. There was a bowl with some dough in it on the kitchen table, as well as a knife and part of a loaf of bread.

PC Bracewell then went back to his house and told the prisoner that he was taking her to Halifax police station, where she would be arrested and charged with the murder of her two children. Meanwhile, surgeon Mr Henry Pritchett was called to the house and he examined the bodies of the two children. He saw that their throats had been cut across, very deeply, and he was certain they would both have died immediately. He went to PC Bracewell's house and asked Mary why she had done it. She told him, 'I've done it and what's done can't be undone.' She gave the same answer to the other questions that he asked her. He noticed that she seemed very dejected, yet restless at the same time; sighing and wringing her hands and walking around the small kitchen. He had asked her if she had enough food and she replied in the affirmative. He then asked her if they were good children and she told him with much feeling, 'Oh yes, little darlings, they were very good.' Accompanied by PCs Bracewell and Ambler, Mary was taken to the train station. She wept on the journey to Halifax and made several references to the fact that she had killed them both. She said that she 'had tried to be like others and I cannot.' PC Bracewell took this to mean that she was referring to the state of the house, which was very poorly furnished. Throughout the journey she was agitated, wringing her hands and appearing to be quite wild.

On Friday, 15 April 1864, an inquest was held into the murders of Mary and Archibald, and the first to give evidence was William Dyson, who displayed obvious signs of anxiety and shock. He told the deputy coroner, Mr Ingram, that he and his wife had been on very good terms and that they had had no rows or quarrels in recent months. He described his wife as being an affectionate mother and said there was no reason to suspect that she wanted to murder the children. The coroner asked him if he was aware of any of his wife's family being insane; Dyson believed so, but could not say for sure. One of the jury asked him if his wife was addicted to alcohol but he refuted this, saying that she had signed the pledge at eight years of age and had kept to it ever since. He did say that for the past month she had been complaining that her head hurt, and that she had seemed to be very confused in the way she spoke to him sometimes. The coroner asked Mary if she had any questions to ask her husband but she replied in the negative. The next to give evidence were PCs Bracewell and Ambler, who described the events which led to the discovery of the two little bodies. PC Ambler caused a sensation in the court when he produced the razor, which still had blood on it. The surgeon, Mr Henry Pritchett, gave his evidence and described performing the initial examination on the bodies and Mrs Dyson's responses to his questions.

The wife of the farmer with whom Mr and Mrs Dyson had previously lodged, Lydia Aspinall, then gave her evidence and told the coroner that the couple had lived with her and her husband from August until they moved to Ogden Lane on 9 April. She had thought on at least two occasions that Mary's mind was not always 'right'. She had talked to Lydia about weird dreams she had been having, and said that she was convinced something would happen to her husband. She worried about what would become of them as a family if he was to have an accident. In reply to a question put to her by the coroner, Mrs Aspinall stated that Mary had never wished to return back to Ireland, mentioning that she had said, 'There are twenty comforts here [in England] to where there was one in Ireland.' Mrs Aspinall went on to tell the jury that Mr and Mrs Dyson had always seemed, to her at least, to be on good terms with each other and that the prisoner had always appeared to be an affectionate mother towards her two children.

The coroner then asked Mary if she had any questions to put to the witness, but she again replied in the negative. He then asked her if she had anything to say and she replied, 'All that has been said is true.'

The coroner then summed up the evidence for the jury. He told them that at this stage they had no need to inquire into the state of mind of the prisoner, as that was a matter for experts elsewhere – all that they had to conclude was how these children came to their deaths. The coroner told them that he recognised it was a fearful case but the evidence was quite clear and he felt that the jury could have no difficulty in arriving at their verdict. The prisoner had admitted that the evidence was true and that she alone had murdered the children. The jury returned with a verdict of wilful murder and she was then taken to the Halifax county police office and charged at noon with murder.

On Saturday 17 April, Mary was brought before the West Riding justices at Halifax Magistrates' Court. The evidence from the witnesses and her own confession left the jury in no doubt that she was guilty and ordered her to take trial at the next York Assizes. She told the chaplain of

Halifax Magistrates' Court, where Mary appeared on 17 April 1864.

the prison that she had intended to do away with herself after killing the children, but when she put the razor down in order to lay the children on the floor she had been horrified at her actions; she could not pick up the instrument and went to give herself up to the police at Rastrick instead.

Mary Ann Dyson stood trial at the assizes at Leeds Town Hall on 16 August 1864 in front of Mr Justice Keating. Mr Middleton conducted the prosecution and the prisoner was defended by Mr Blackburn. Mary's father, Archibald Thompson, was a surprise witness at the assizes. He spoke about their life in Ireland and described how Dyson came to live with them, and how he had fallen in love with his daughter. He said that when she was little, Mary was subject to fits because of a spinal injury.

'she had been horrified at her actions'

When she was old enough to earn a wage she was put to work as an apprentice milliner, but he had to fetch her home as she was constantly complaining of weakness and feeling unwell. He had once found her in a very distressed state, having thrown herself in the waters of the River Shannon. On another occasion she ran away from home without any clothes on and was not found until the following day. Her father described his daughter as being very eccentric in her habits and that her brother and sisters had all suffered from a disease of the brain – four of them had died of this cause.

Mary's mother also attended and she confirmed much of the evidence given by her husband. The surgeon, Mr Pritchett, was called and he stated that as four of her siblings had died from disease of the brain it was obvious that the prisoner would show a tendency towards insanity.

Mary appeared at the Assizes at Leeds Town Hall on 16 August 1864.

He gave his opinion that the prisoner was subject to impulsive insanity. The judge asked him to clarify if she was incapable of judging what was right or wrong, and the surgeon replied that, 'There might be some dim consciousness of it, without the power to control the action.' He said that when he visited her on the day after the murder, the prisoner appeared to be wild and insane. Mr Pritchett once again asked her why she had done it and she told him that she couldn't tell him anything other than that the thought had come upon her so she did it. He gave his opinion that when the prisoner committed the murder she was insane.

The prosecution disagreed and told the jury that nothing in Mary's conduct justified the conclusion that she was insane, apart from her obvious distress at having taken the lives of her two children. He felt that the evidence of her parents had amounted to nothing more than acts of eccentricity or waywardness. The judge summed up and stated that:

> Of all the mysterious afflictions which was visited on humanity, this was the most mysterious, the most inscrutable, the most various in its mani-festations and the way in which it developed itself. But although this was so, I can only put the question to the jury in the way in which it was sanc-tioned by law. That is whether at the time when the prisoner committed this act, if she knew the difference between right and wrong. If you are satisfied of that, then you will find the prisoner guilty of wilful murder. If you believe and are satisfied that she was not able to distinguish between right and wrong, it will be your duty to say that she was not guilty on the grounds of insanity.

The jury was absent for only twenty minutes before returning a verdict that she was not guilty on the grounds of insanity. The judge then ordered Mary Dyson to be detained at Her Majesty's pleasure.

CASE SIX 1864

A CANAL SIDE RESCUE

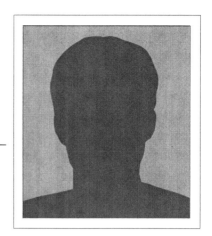

Suspect: Thomas Drake
Age: Eighteen
Charge: Attempted Murder
Sentence: Penal Servitude

The Calder and Hebble Navigation Canal runs through Halifax and was built as an extension to the Calder and Aire Canal in order to bring goods from Wakefield to Sowerby Bridge. Canals were the early transport routes of the Victorian era and it was not long before they were transporting heavy materials such as coal and timber. However, canals were also used as pathways for families and courting couples.

The Calder and Hebble Canal, which runs through Halifax.

On Tuesday, 6 December 1864, Eliza Wilson, who was described as having a very youthful appearance – she was only seventeen years of age – was late for work. Without having breakfast, she left her lodgings on Nelson Street and made her way to the silk mill in Halifax where she worked. However, when Eliza arrived she was turned away by the foreman for being a few minutes late – it was one of the rules of the mill that an hour's pay was docked off the day's wages for anyone who was late. As a result of this, Eliza decided to go home and have some breakfast before returning to work.

On her way home she was met by Thomas Drake, who suggested that they take a walk by the canal, to which she agreed. Thomas was aged eighteen and a dyer at the same mill. Despite their young age the couple had previously lived together as man and wife before they had argued and she had left him and gone to stay in lodgings. As they walked along Drake tried to persuade her to come back to him, but she was reluctant and told him that she wouldn't. At Caddy Lane Bridge the canal path sloped downwards towards the water. As they walked towards it, down the slope, suddenly and without any provocation, Drake seized Eliza around the waist and threw her into the canal. After callously watching her struggle for a few moments, Drake heard two women shout to some men that there was a girl in the water. He ran off to hide in a nearby lumberyard.

John Furness, a stone cutter who had been working near to the canal that morning, heard the women shout out that there was a woman in the canal. Running to the bridge he saw Eliza struggling in the water, before she disappeared just under the bridge. By now Furness was almost at the canal side, pulling off his coat as he ran. When he reached the spot where Eliza had gone under he jumped into the water. He dived down to the bottom of the canal but it was so dark that he could not see or feel anything, but, undaunted, he dived down again. Finally he succeeded in bringing the unfortunate girl to the surface and two of his workmates pulled her out of the water, although she was barely conscious. He later said that he was so exhausted himself that if his friends had not been at the side of the canal, he would have been unable to get both himself and the girl out and would probably have sunk with her.

At this point, Drake reappeared at the side of the canal and promptly threw himself into the water so that the two men, who were now looking after the girl, were forced to help him out of the canal as well. Even after he had been rescued, Drake struggled to throw himself back into the water. The men took the still struggling Drake and the exhausted girl to the nearby

'she was barely conscious'

Ship Inn and a constable was summoned. Drake, rather than showing any gratitude towards his rescuers, attacked them at the inn, shouting that they should have left him to drown. The constable arrived and Drake was taken into custody before being taken to the Borough Court. Later that day, Drake was brought before the Bench, charged with the attempted murder of Eliza Wilson, who, by now, had recovered sufficiently to give evidence. The magistrate, in the summing up for the jury, praised the courage of Furness in his rescue of Drake and Eliza. The jury took only minutes to find Drake guilty and ordered that he stand trial at the next assizes.

On Friday 23 December at the Leeds Assizes, Drake appeared before Mr Justice Keaton. The first witness was Eliza Wilson, who described the ordeal on the canal side and her rescue by John Furness. The judge asked 3er what her relationship was like with Drake prior to the incident and she

Leeds Assizes courtroom, where Drake appeared on 23 December 1864.

told him that they had lived well enough together and that he had been quite kind to her. John Furness was the next witness and he explained how he had been told that there was a young woman in the canal, before describing his brave rescue. The judge praised him for his courage and told him:

> Mr Furness, I wish to tell you that you have behaved in a most gallant and creditable manner and you deserve the thanks of everybody who knows you. If I had the power I would order you to be so rewarded, but I much regret that I do not have that power.

Another witness, George Robertshaw, stated that he had seen the prisoner standing close to the water watching the girl struggle. He then saw him run towards the timber yard and disappear. Robertshaw saw Furness rescue the girl and he went to help pull her out of the water. He described the way that Drake had reappeared again and tried to throw himself into the canal. He had helped another man to pull Drake out, but had met with great resistance and he struggled with them all the way to the Ship Inn, where he struck out at them both. Another witness was eleven-year-old Caroline Pratt, who had passed the couple just as Drake put his arms around Eliza and threw her into the canal. Pratt described that within a second or two of passing them she heard a splash and a scream and, turning, saw Eliza in the water.

Drake's defence lawyer, Mr Wheelhouse, stated that beyond the girl's evidence, which he suggested was not worthy of credence, there was nothing to show that Drake was guilty of the crime with which he was charged. Eliza had not supplied any motive, apart from the slight quarrel she had with the prisoner, and he suggested that it was more probable that the girl had tripped and fallen into the water. He then went on to inform the jury that Drake had an accident three years ago – he was thrown from a horse and since then he had been subject to fits. Although the fits had become less regular, he was still prone to periods of what he called 'light states'.

His grandfather and mother appeared before the Bench, accompanied by the woman with whom Drake had lodged. All three of them stated that they had witnessed the fits and the repercussions. His mother told the judge that on the night before the incident, he had had a fit which lasted for over an hour and left him feeling light-headed for the rest of the day. Mr Wheelhouse maintained that if he had thrown the girl into the water he was not responsible for his own actions.

The judge summed up the evidence for the jury and he seemed horrified by the fact that the young couple had lived together as man and wife for a few short months. He commented on the lamentable state of morality which had been exposed by Miss Wilson, 'without the least hesitation or apparent shame'. He condemned the fact that, at only seventeen years of age, she seemed to think that that such behaviour was an ordinary rule of life. The jury took only half an hour before delivering the verdict that Drake was guilty of attempted murder. In passing sentence the judge said:

> The jury have convicted you of one of the most serious offenses, short of murder, that can be committed, because they have found that you threw this young girl into the canal intending to murder her. It is an offence which is sometimes properly punishable with the severest sentence that the law admits. That sentence would extend to penal servitude for the remainder of your days, but I hope, in consideration of your youth and some other circumstances connected with this prosecution, that I am justified, consistently with my duty, in passing upon you a lesser sentence, although it must be a terribly severe one. The sentence of the court is that you be kept in penal servitude for the term of fifteen years.

Showing little remorse for his actions, Drake was led down beneath the court to the cells.

CASE SEVEN   1865

CHILD MURDER

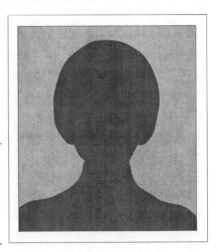

Suspect: Janet Currie
Age: Thirty
Charge: Murder
Sentence: Discharged

In Victorian society, to bring an illegitimate child into the world was frowned upon. There are hundreds of cases of newborn babies being found in the towns and cities of the West Riding, in rivers and canals, on rubbish heaps and privies. Indeed, it is thought by modern historians that this gruesome act might have been some primitive form of birth control.

A case was brought to the attention of the Halifax authorities by a woman who had been charged with the concealment of birth and the killing of her child, not just once but four times. On 10 December 1865, a thirty-year-old spinster from Scotland, named Janet Currie, was charged with killing her child, before being placed in a cell.

She was brought before the Magistrates' Court at Halifax the next day, where she was described as a domestic servant. She had been employed for some time at Mr North's commercial eating house on Northgate, Halifax, as a cook. Mr North's wife had accused her of being pregnant but she had always denied it.

It seems that on the morning in question Mrs North saw Currie lying on her bedroom floor and thought that the way she was laying looked suspicious. She informed her husband, who was not very well at the time – as a consequence of his illness a search was not undertaken until later on the same day. Mrs North discovered the hiding place when the baby started to cry. A newly-born infant had been wrapped up in a hearthrug, and was found under the cellar steps. Mr North, on hearing what had taken place, came down into the kitchen and fell into a passion, telling Currie that she had to leave. He hailed her a cab and she brought the child, wrapped in cloths, out of the cellar and left the premises.

At her request, the cab dropped her off in Horton Street. She walked around the centre of Halifax for some time before going into an eating house owned by a woman named Mrs Marion Lord. Using some of her meagre amount of money, Currie ordered some tea and bread and butter. After finishing her meal she then wandered around the town until it was dark, pondering how she was to get out of this dilemma. About 9 p.m. she went to the Railway Hotel on Horton Street, which was owned by Mrs Bolton, and asked for a bed for the night for herself and the child. Mrs Bolton saw that she looked ill and gave her a room, asking one of the servants, a girl named Helen Smith, to keep an eye on her. Around noon the following day, Helen saw Currie taking the child out of the house and the servant girl noted that the baby was a healthy little girl.

The Railway Hotel on Horton Street, Halifax, where Janet asked for a bed for the night for herself and her child.

In the course of the afternoon, Currie was spotted walking backwards and forwards across Caddy Lane Bridge, where she was seen at around four o'clock by two witnesses; a man named James Thorp and a man named Robertshaw. Thorp, seeing the bundle in her arms, decided to follow Currie at a discreet distance. Around 5.15 p.m. they saw that she was walking by the canal near Hebble Brook, which was opposite the entrance to Messrs Robert Crossley & Sons Mills. The two men followed her back to Mrs Lord's eating house, where once again she had some more refreshment. After finishing her meal, Currie continued walking up and down along the same canal side. On several occasions the two men, who had now been joined by a third named Seth Wood, watched her demonstrating her agitation by looking into the lock and several times walking away again. Finally, after seeing her do this once more, the three men saw her throw the bundle she had been carrying into the canal. Hearing the sound of a child's cry, Currie was seized by Thorp and accused of throwing the child into the water. He told her that he was going to fetch a policeman and she told him that if he did, she would throw herself into the canal. Thorp left her in the charge of his companions, instructing them not to let her go, and went to fetch a police constable. It would appear that there was no effort to try to rescue the child from the canal.

The constable arrived and Currie was taken to the Town Hall. A search of the canal was made and the child's body was found wrapped up in a man's waistcoat. It had drifted into a dam further downstream. The prisoner was examined by surgeon Mr Wright shortly after she was taken into custody, and it was confirmed that she had recently given birth. On the same day that the child's body was found, Currie was arrested in her cell in front of the magistrate, Mr James Bowman, and was charged with murder.

When the police investigated further into the case, it was found that, two years previously, Currie had been charged with the same offence while living at the same establishment, which was then owned by a Mr Vickers. Four years previously a similar offence had been dismissed in the Magistrates' Court, and on another occasion Currie was taken to the assizes, where she had been sentenced to three months' imprisonment for the same offence.

The inquest into the death of the child took place the following afternoon at the Town Hall before Mr Dyson, the coroner. The prisoner was still in a very weak state following her ordeal and was permitted to lie on a day bed, which had been fitted up in the coroner's court. Throughout the inquest she made no remarks and looked extremely pale. Various witnesses spoke about seeing her with the child and acting in a very suspicious manner. After listening to Mr North, the coroner castigated him for the callous treatment he showed his former employee and for turning her and the child out onto the streets after she had recently given birth. He advised Mr North that he should have exercised greater consideration. He also criticised the three men, Thorp, Robertshaw and Wood, for following her around but not trying to help her or prevent her from throwing the child into the canal. He told them that in all his experience as a coroner he had met nothing like it and that although there was no law to punish them, they certainly were not guiltless. The jury, after just twenty-five minutes of consultation, returned a verdict of wilful murder. They also added their concurrence of the coroner's remarks with regards to North, Thorp, Robertshaw and Wood.

Currie was brought before Mr Justice Shee at the Leeds Assizes on Tuesday, 9 January 1866, charged with the murder of her child. The prisoner had no defence and at the request of the judge a solicitor named Mr Foster agreed to act for her.

When Mr North gave his evidence and spoke about ejecting her from his house, he was also reprimanded by the judge, who told him:

That was not the way, Sir, to treat a woman under such circumstances. Nobody would find fault with the father of a family, or a person having a young woman about him, for expressing his displeasure to the woman who had a child under such circumstances in his house. But turning her out, letting her go out, although willing, in such a condition, just after she had been delivered, without sending for a medical man, or any decent respectable woman to take care of her, is not the right course.

Mr North appeared to be filled with virtuous indignation towards the prisoner as he bristled at the judge's words. He protested that she did not go out without his consent, to which the judge replied, 'You fetched a cab instead of fetching somebody to look after her. You should not have done that.' When Mr North tried to protest once more, saying, 'Well, my Lord...' the judge cut him off, saying, 'That is enough.'

The next witness to take the stand was Mr Thorp, who was asked by Mr Foster why, when following Currie around the canal side, he did not try to speak to her or to try to prevent her from throwing the child in the canal. He replied, 'Well, Sir, we thought we had better not do so. We thought if we did, we should be charged with taking indecent liberties with her.' Unbelievably he had now changed his story and maintained that although they had heard that she had recently given birth to a child, they had followed her not to watch her throw the child into the canal, but rather that they thought she was going to meet someone on the canal tow path.

Mr Wright, the surgeon who had performed the post-mortem on the child, confirmed that the cause of death had been drowning, as the child's lungs were filled with water and particles of mud. He stated that there was no perceptible difference in the effects of suffocation in water and suffocation out of water. He informed the court that if the child had been suffocated before being thrown into the water there would have been no mud in the lungs. He confidently stated that childbirth frequently caused women to be affected mentally and that the consequent exposure to cold and fatigue, so soon after confinement, would probably lead to light-headedness. In his opinion the prisoner would probably have committed the act because the balance of her mind was disrupted.

Mr Foster, in Currie's defence, told the judge that this was one of the most painful cases he had ever had to defend. He pointed out that his client had acted as honourably as she could under the circumstances. When her master had suspected that she had given birth, he bundled her into a cab without any money to procure her daily bread – she was left to go where she could. He stated that, 'On the streets of Halifax she went from place to place with her child, receiving no sympathy and her scanty means diminishing. This woman was exposed to all the rigours of winter weather without any of the comforts that even the beasts of the fields were accustomed to.' Mr Foster then described, in detail, the anguish of her walk by the canal:

Gazing into the water again and again, trying to summon up the courage to commit this dreadful act. I do not know her true thoughts but was it possible that instead of killing the child she was contemplating her own destruction. I don't want to disparage the witnesses who had watched her, but it would have been better for them to have told their suspicions to the police when they first saw her, and who would have, in the course of his duty, taken her to the workhouse. If that had been done she would have found a roof over her and the baby's head and food to eat. Instead, on that wretched Sunday, they chose to follow her about until towards evening, when she probably experienced that lightness of head and diminished responsibility, of which the surgeon had spoken, and she took the action she did. Indeed, by this time the child might have already been dead in her arms, suffocated as she tried to hold it close to her breast in order to keep it warm. I suppose that if she discovered the child was dead in her arms, she might then have suffered from such light-headedness that she threw away the dead body into the black water which would get into the child's lungs and deposit the mud wherever it went.

Concluding his eloquent defence, Mr Foster pointed out that if this was indeed the turn of events it would still have been an unlawful act but a lesser one, one of concealment of birth, and the offence would be manslaughter rather than murder.

The judge summed up for the jury, stating that if they thought the prisoner had been in such a frame of mind, resulting in her not knowing her actions, then they must give a verdict of manslaughter not murder. He once again castigated Mr North for his harsh treatment of Currie, turning her out without so much as the last few days wages which she had already earned. He told the jury that married women of comfortable means sometimes lost their reason for a time following childbirth and, therefore, they cease being accountable for their actions. It was much more to be expected that a woman in Currie's circumstances should be in such a state of mind. The jury took only forty minutes to return a verdict of not guilty, proclaiming Janet Currie a free woman.

SOLVED

CASE EIGHT 1865

DEATH OF A SISTER

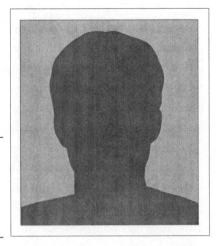

Suspect: Thomas Cockcroft
Age: Forty-two
Charge: Murder
Sentence: Life Imprisonment

Thomas Cockcroft, aged forty-two, was a farm labourer who had lived with his sister, Hannah Helliwell, at Sowerby for the last five years. Henry Helliwell, Hannah's son, also resided in the same house, along with her daughter Sarah and her granddaughter, Sarah-Anne, who was aged about eight years.

On the morning of 20 June 1865, Henry, Sarah and Sarah-Anne left the house to go to their respective duties, leaving Cockcroft and Hannah at home. When Sarah-Anne returned home from school for lunch she discovered her grandmother lying injured on the floor. A neighbour, James Farrar, was called to the house. When he arrived he was shocked to see Hannah lying on the floor in a pool of blood; her head and face were covered in blood, her jaw was broken and he found that she was barely alive. There was no sign of Thomas Cockcroft.

A surgeon, Mr James Horsfall of Sowerby Bridge, was quickly summoned and Hannah was moved to the hospital where she survived until the 27th, but she never regained consciousness. It seems that the wounds had been inflicted by a pair of tongs which were usually kept in the kitchen. The family later confirmed to the police that they had been there in the morning but following the murder were missing.

On the same day of the attack, Amos Taylor saw Cockcroft crouching down between stone walls which surrounded a nearby field. Another witness, Joseph Naylor, spotted him at about 2 p.m. at a further distance from the house. News that he was a wanted man had reached Naylor, who said to him, 'What hast thou been doing at Sowerby?' Cockcroft told him that Hannah had wanted to mend his waistcoat. He had objected to her doing so unless she used new cotton, but when she refused he hit her. He told Naylor that he had not meant to hit her but once he had started he could not stop. He had given two or three blows to her face and then kicked at her with his clogs before he attacked her with the iron tongs, which he threw away as he made his escape.

'once he had started he could not stop'

Naylor and Taylor gave information of Cockcroft's whereabouts to the police authorities and at 4 p.m. Cockcroft was found and brought to Halifax Town Hall. In the meantime, the tongs which he had used to kill his sister had been found, bent and twisted out of shape. Two days after Mrs Helliwell's death, 29 June, an inquest was held at the Kings Head Inn at Sowerby. A post-mortem examination had been conducted by Mr Horsfall and he was of the opinion that the principal injuries had been inflicted with the tongs. The following day, the prisoner was brought before the magistrates at Halifax, where the jury found him guilty and sentenced him to stand trial at the next assizes.

Cockcroft was brought to the Leeds Assizes on Wednesday, 9 August 1865, before the judge, Mr Justice Mellor. He was described as a sedate-looking man who pleaded guilty. When the judge asked him point blank if he had intended to murder his sister, he said that he had hit her but he never intended to murder her. The judge sought to clarify the issue and asked him, 'Did you attack her with malice aforethought, that is with an intention to kill her?' At this Cockcroft shook his head vigorously and told the judge that he did it in a passion, and after a consultation with another judge, a not guilty plea was recorded accordingly.

The first witness to take the stand was Henry Helliwell, who said that he left the house at 6.45 a.m. to go to work, leaving his mother in bed. He said that his uncle had been subject to fits of despondency and depression for many years and was often in such low spirits that he would take to his

Halifax Town Hall, where Cockroft was brought on 20 June 1865.

bed for days on end. On such occasions he would stare wildly and hardly blinked or spoke to anyone. For a fortnight before the murder he had been in very low spirits and had refused to go to work. Henry stated that before the attack, he had never known his uncle to use violence on anyone, let alone his own sister.

James Horsfall, the surgeon, declared that he had been called to see Hannah on the day of the attack and he described the injuries which the poor woman had sustained. He said that the wounds had been inflicted with great violence and that some of the wounds were so deep that they went down to the skull. He had no doubt that these wounds were the cause of her death. Horsfall was questioned very carefully as to whether, in his opinion, the prisoner had acted whilst labouring under monomania, to which he replied in the affirmative.

Another surgeon, Mr W.N. Price, was then examined. He stated that while Cockcroft had been imprisoned he had had the opportunity to closely observe the prisoner on several occasions and as part of this observation had been given the opportunity to talk to Cockcroft. He gave his opinion that the prisoner was of a very low type and a very ignorant man, but that he had not seen any indications of insanity. Mr Price also stated that he could see little evidence of any disease of the brain and that on occasions Cockcroft appeared to be cool and collected. He then informed the judge that he had heard evidence indicative of all the classic symptoms of deep depression, but that he had heard nothing which would point towards homicidal mania. The surgeon said he would be cautious in such cases, but would not ordinarily assign the prisoner to an asylum. He also clarified that, 'The depression to which he was subject to might result in an act of fury, in which state he would not, during the fit, know the moral consequences of his actions.'

The prosecution summed up the evidence and contended that although the prisoner was sullen and sometimes low-spirited, he knew perfectly well what he was doing at the time of the murder. The defence countered the argument by highlighting the fact that there were other cases of insanity in the prisoner's family and that Cockcroft had been subject to fits of depression, in which he manifested irrational conduct and was prone to sullen outbursts of passion. The act of the prisoner in this case showed to be utterly without reason and without motive. He concluded that the prisoner had been labouring under a form of homicidal monomania at the time of the murder and therefore was not responsible for his actions. In such a case, as he had made the attack without any intention of committing murder, he should not be charged with murder but rather the lesser crime of manslaughter. The judge summed up the evidence for the jury, telling them:

You must consider the whole circumstances of the case, and return such a verdict as you, in your conscience and in accordance with the oath you have taken, believe to be right. If a man was truly labouring under such mental disease that made him not know what he was doing, then the verdict would be one of not guilty on the grounds of insanity. If you consider that the circumstances of the case should prove that there had been some provocation, so as to reduce the offence to that of manslaughter, you should return a verdict to that effect. But if you believe that the prisoner knew what he was doing, and that the offence with which he was charged was the result of uncontrolled passion and bad temper, it is your duty to find him guilty of murder.

After an absence of almost two hours, the jury returned with a verdict of guilty with a strong recommendation to mercy. The judge, in a brief but solemn address, told Cockcroft that he was guilty of a murder committed against his own sister and under circumstances of great brutality. He then sentenced the prisoner to be hanged by the neck until he was dead. The prisoner left the dock looking unmoved by the judge's words.

A week later, news was heard that the Home Secretary, Sir George Grey, had commuted Cockcroft's sentence to life imprisonment because of the jury's recommendation to mercy. Mr Justice Mellor expressed his concurrence with the decision.

CASE NINE 1868

MURDER AT THE PARSONAGE

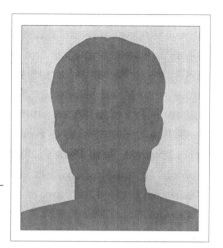

Suspect: Miles Weatherill
Age: Twenty-three
Charge: Murder
Sentence: Execution

Miles Weatherill, aged twenty-three, lived in Todmorden, where he regularly attended the local church and was a Sunday school teacher. He was described as respectable, hard working and as having a slightly above average intelligence. It was said that when he finished his day's work as a weaver, he was often found to be in the news and reading rooms in

The Parsonage at Todmorden as it is today.

town catching up on local and national news. Weatherill was the only son of a widowed mother and had a sister of a similar age. He lived a well-ordered life until he met and fell in love with Sarah Bell. She was the servant of the local vicar, Reverend Plow, and worked at the parsonage in Todmorden. In an attempt to win over her employer, he asked Revd Plow's permission to court Sarah. After some discussion with his wife, however, Revd Plow declined his request, for reasons which never became absolutely clear. His honourable attempt to court Sarah foiled, Weatherill decided to resort to murder.

On Monday, 2 March 1868, Revd Plow had been out on church visits between 8.15 p.m. and 9.40 p.m. and upon returning home had some supper with his wife before he rang for prayers, which were held each evening with all his family and staff. Another servant girl named Jane Smith entered the room and informed Revd Plow that she had seen Weatherill outside the back door. She told the Revd that he wished to speak with him so he went to the back door, where he saw Weatherill waiting for him. Without speaking, Weatherill raised a pistol which he had been

The back door to the Parsonage at Todmorden, where Jane Smith informed Revd Plow that Miles Weatherill was waiting.

holding at his side. Before the Revd could call out or move away Weatherill pointed it at his head and fired. Thankfully, the cap exploded but the pistol did not go off. However, undaunted by this, Weatherill drew out an axe from behind his back. When Revd Plow moved to grab Weatherill by the neck, he struck the clergyman on the head twice. By now there was a great deal of blood and the poor man loudly shouted out 'Murder!'

'the poor man loudly shouted out "Murder!"'

Still struggling along the passage away from the parsonage's back door, Weatherill continued to beat Revd Plow's head with the axe. Three servants were now in the passage as well, including Jane Smith, who went towards the two struggling men and grabbed hold of Weatherill in order to try to take the axe from him. But just as the two men were opposite the dining room door Weatherill drew out another pistol, put it to Revd Plow's ear and pulled the trigger. Once again, unbelievably, the pistol did not fire and the clergyman wrestled it from his grasp. Turning his attention to Jane Smith, Weatherill struck at her twice on the head with the axe and she ran screaming into the dining room. The woman put her back against the dining room door in an attempt to deter Weatherill, who was loudly accusing her of telling tales to her master about his visits to see Sarah. Finally managing to push the door open he shot her dead with another pistol.

While Weatherill was attacking Jane Smith, the Revd took the chance to escape and ran out of the front door with a pistol in his hand. After Weatherill had shot Jane Smith he closely pursued Revd Plow, drawing another pistol from his belt and firing at the clergyman once more. The servants inside the house heard two more shots ring out, but Revd Plow had managed to escape to a neighbour's house.

Meanwhile, inside the house, the servants had taken cover. Margaret Bell, the nurse who had been attending Mrs Plow during her recent childbirth, watched Weatherill from her mistress's bedroom upstairs. She saw him walk between the front room and the kitchen and noticed that he was loading a pistol. She then looked on in horror as he came upstairs carrying the pistol

The path leading to the back door of Todmorden Parsonage, along which neighbours walked to rescue Revd Plow.

in one hand and the kitchen poker in the other. Bell ran into the bedroom of Mrs Plow and, because there was no lock, put her back to the door in an attempt to prevent him from entering. He told her, 'Let me in, I mean you no harm,' and pushed at the door with all his might. Overcoming Bell, he managed to get inside the bedroom; she pleaded for him to take mercy upon them and begged him not to harm the newborn baby. Weatherill remained silent as he approached the bed in which Mrs Plow lay.

Mrs Bell heard neighbours, who had heard Revd Plow's pleas, hammering at the front door trying to gain entrance. She ran downstairs to let them in, but found the front door locked and the key missing. Eventually, a Mr Stansfield and others were admitted through the back door of the parsonage. They heard shots ring out from the bedroom and rushed upstairs to find Mrs Plow on the bed, blood running from her nose and forehead, saturating her clothes. Weatherill had attempted to shoot Mrs Plow but had missed, so he had resorted to beating her over the head with a poker.

Mr Stansfield and another neighbour, Mr Charles Edward Binks, captured Weatherill as he rushed out of the bedroom. Stansfield asked the captured man if he knew that he had killed Jane Smith, to which he replied, 'Yes, and if it hadn't been for the bloody pistols there would have been two more deaths here tonight.' Weatherill showed no remorse or fear when he was taken downstairs to wait for the police to arrive, he calmly took out his pipe and lit it, saying, 'I may as well have a smoke; I suppose it is the last I shall have, for I know I will swing for what I have done.' The police arrived shortly afterwards and on searching Weatherill found that he was wearing a home-made pistol belt which was tied at the back with string. Four holes had been made in the belt, into which the four pistols had been inserted. In his pockets they found a quantity of gunpowder, many bullets and caps and some loose shot.

In his statement, Weatherill said that the reason for the attempted murder was to gain revenge on Revd Plow for his objection to seeing Sarah. Revd Plow had asked her to stop seeing Weatherill, but when the relationship continued he accused his servant of a breach of trust, and as a consequence she was dismissed by Mrs Plow. Weatherill claimed that by dismissing Sarah he had taken away her character and she would be unable to find further employment. After Weatherill threatened the Reverend, the clergyman took steps to prevent him from intruding on the grounds. Despite his fears, the girl was given a good reference by Mr and Mrs Plow and Sarah quickly found work at the Friends Retreat, an asylum in York where Weatherill visited her on the Saturday and Sunday before the attack.

On Wednesday 4 March, the inquest into Jane Smith's death was undertaken by the coroner, at which Weatherill was present. He was described as a young man who was considered to be quite good looking. The prisoner appeared to be unconcerned during the proceedings and laughed and conversed with the officers in charge of him. He corrected and cross-examined the witnesses, as was his right, and behaved very coolly for a man in such a serious position; however, he appeared to be more thoughtful when Revd Plow gave his evidence. Weatherill had told the policeman who arrested him that if he had not been collared he would have made his escape to Hebden Bridge that night. After hearing all the evidence the jury found him guilty of wilful murder.

On Friday 6 March, the case was heard at the Magistrates' Court in Todmorden at 3 p.m. The court and the approaches to it were crowded long before the appointed hour of the case, and it was with extreme difficulty that the magistrates and witnesses were able to obtain an entrance. The prisoner had no defence, but he seemed to take a great interest in the evidence and took copious notes throughout the proceedings. He was placed between two police constables and, according to the journalists reporting on the case, appeared young and small in stature with a reddish moustache. Despite his boyish appearance, the five charges made against him were very serious:

Murder of Jane Smith
Attempting to shoot Revd Anthony John Plow with intent to murder him
Feloniously wounding Revd Plow with intent to murder him
Shooting at Mrs Harriet Louisa Plow with intent to murder her
Feloniously striking her with a poker, with intent to murder her

Despite his brave demeanour it was reported that his countenance changed while listening to the details of his crime, especially when the bloody axe was produced in the courtroom.

Great sympathy was shown to Revd Plow, who was the first to take the stand as a witness. It was evident that he was still in a feeble and exhausted state. He told the court that he was the vicar of Todmorden and that Sarah Bell had been in his service from 1864, first as a nurse then, in the second year of her employment at the parsonage, she became the cook. She was a very valued and important member of his staff, until she started an acquaintance with Weatherill. He announced that Mrs Plow was unable to attend due to the severity of her injuries and that her health was in a most precarious state. Revd Plow said that when Weatherill had asked permission to court Sarah Bell, he had told him that he did not approve of long courtships happening under his roof, but at the same time complemented him on his straightforwardness and honesty. He described how, one evening, he heard shots being fired at his back door; he later found out that it was covered in shot and the window was broken. At this point, the prisoner asked Revd Plow why he had denied permission for the relationship to continue even though he knew that Sarah's parents had approved of the courtship. Revd Plow told him that it was mainly because the girl was so young and that even though Weatherill showed good intentions towards the girl, he just didn't trust him. The clergyman stated that he had been under the impression that the affair had been over for six months before he found out that Sarah Bell had lied to himself and his wife and that she had continued to see Weatherill.

The prisoner watched him impassively as he gave his evidence and, indeed, the only time he displayed any emotion was when he was listening to the evidence of his sweetheart, Sarah Bell. She was described as being a very interesting, good-looking girl who was very affected by the evidence she was giving. Sarah was asked if Weatherill had asked her to marry him, to which she coolly replied that it referred to a private matter and had nothing to do with the case. Some letters between the prisoner and Sarah were read out, which indicated that he had asked her to come and live back in Todmorden once more. He had written to her, stating that to walk out together would plague the Plows more. One of the letters read:

We should not have had any occasion to be parted at all had Plow been a gentleman. He and his wife and the traitor [Jane Smith] have spoiled our happiness, and unless that happiness can be renewed they shall rue it; for I will open Jane's secret to all Todmorden, and [we] will not be the only ones to suffer. No; the traitor will suffer a little. I cannot forgive them for doing what they have done, because we acted honourably, and it was not right of them to do as they have.

Sarah told the court that the Revd Plow had found out about the deception and she left their employ on 12 November. On that date, Weatherill had accompanied her to her home at Newby Wiske, near Thirsk, and he had stayed with her for two or three days. Once she had been given the position at York he had also visited her there. During his visit she told him that Jane Smith had been telling tales to the Revd Plow about his visits and he vowed that he would have his revenge on her, although he did not state what form of revenge it would be.

Medical evidence and a description of Revd Plow's injuries were given by the surgeon, Dr Foot. He described that the Reverend had several deep wounds on his head and his left ear was split in two. The doctor stated that Mrs Plow's injuries were also extremely severe; the bone of her nose was broken and her head was cut in several places. The jury found Miles

'his left ear was split in two'

Weatherill guilty and he was committed to the Manchester Assizes to take his trial. At the dismissal of the court, Sarah Bell went up to Weatherill and embraced him for the last time.

Despite the fact that the proceedings had taken most of the day (they finished at 9.30 p.m.), the police were unable to remove the prisoner due to the crowds' refusal to disperse, and it was with great difficulty that he was finally removed from the courthouse.

The funeral of Jane Smith took place later the same day and was attended by a large concourse of people. She was buried in the church-yard of the parish church, which adjoins the parsonage; her grave was only about twenty yards away from the spot where she was murdered.

Todmorden parish church, c. 1912.

Shockingly, news was heard on Friday 12 March that Revd Plow died from his injuries. He had died that evening at six o'clock from inflammation of the brain, which was caused by the injuries inflicted on him by Weatherill.

The inquest into Revd Plow's death was heard on Monday 16 March at the Black Swan Inn. The coroner, Mr F. Dearden, announced that a vast amount of rubbish had been reported in the local newspaper and demanded that all reporters leave the inquest, something which was not popular with the jury. Nevertheless, they left and the inquest went ahead. After hearing all the evidence of other witnesses and the statement of the surgeon, the jury returned a verdict of wilful murder against Miles Weatherill. At the close of the inquest, the coroner offered condolences to his widow, Mrs Plow, and the two young children who were left fatherless.

On the day that Revd Plow's death was announced, Weatherill's case opened at the South Lancashire Assizes at Manchester before Mr Justice Lush. When the prosecution announced the death of Revd Plow it seemed to come as some surprise to the prisoner; he pleaded not guilty. The prosecution lawyer, Mr Campbell Foster, who was aware of the notoriety of the case, asked the jury to clear their mind of the sensational nature of the crime and to judge it on the evidence produced in court. Weatherill's defence, Mr Torr, tried to prove that at the time of the murder the prisoner's mind had been affected, which was indicated by the atrocity and manner of the deed. After a lengthy trial, the jury returned a verdict of guilty and the judge passed the sentence of death, dismissing the claim of insanity.

On the Sunday morning following the trial, the assistant curate preached the sermon and it was noted that the entire congregation passed the parsonage on the way to the service. Opposite the eastern end of the church was the grave of Jane Smith and next to it, within ten yards of the church, was an open grave which was to receive the remains of Revd Plow. Prayers were said by the congregation, not only for Revd Plow, but also for Miles Weatherill, who was now lying under sentence of death.

It was announced that the execution would take place at Manchester on Saturday 4 April, where he would be hanged along with another murderer, Timothy Flaherty. Revd Plow's own father asked that a day of prayer and humiliation be offered, stating: 'Lest the vengeance of the

Lord should come upon the congregation for the murder of a priest.' Meanwhile, Weatherill remained unrepentant of his crime. Indeed, it was said within the prison that Weatherill had commanded the chaplain to leave his cell, to take his books with him and to trouble him no more.

Miles Weatherill and Timothy Flaherty were hanged at the New Bailey at Salford at eight o'clock in front of an immense crowd of spectators said to have been between 20,000 and 25,000. It seems that his outburst against the chaplain was forgiven, as Weatherill spent the remainder of his time in prayer with him. Before he was hanged, Weatherill also acknowledged the justice of his sentence. When he appeared on his way to the scaffold he was clutching a prayer book and it was reported that his lips were moving as if he was repeating prayers. Both condemned men were reported to be pale and the gaol chaplain accompanied Weatherill. The chaplain reported that he had repented of his transgressions on the night before his execution.

Weatherall's was one of the last hangings to be held in public. The following month it was decided that all hangings were to take place in

Christ Church, Todmorden. Revd Plow's grave lies to the rear of the church (hidden by the tiles of the lych gate).

private and that a black flag would now be erected in order to show the public that the execution had taken place. The same month, it was announced that the congregation at Todmorden were planning to erect a stained-glass window in the church in memory of their late vicar. The newspapers no doubt exacerbated the excitement in the case, but there is no denying that many were completely stunned by the viciousness of the attack inflicted by such a cold, calculated killer.

SOLVED

CASE TEN   1870

MURDERED BY HIS SON

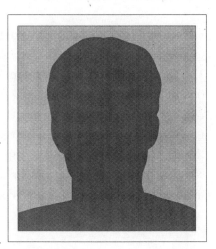

Suspect:	Walter Crabtree
Age:	Forty-nine
Charge:	Murder
Sentence:	Not Guilty

The early Victorians were great newspaper readers, avid for news of what was happening in the local area as well as in the towns and cities of Great Britain. As the century went on more people had access to education and many taught themselves to read from the newspapers of the time. Morning newspapers were usually delivered by early trains and so towns like Halifax would be able to read about the goings-on of the metropolis with their breakfast. For those who got their newspaper in December 1870, they would read about a shocking murder which happened in their own town.

William Crabtree, a widower aged forty-nine, was a printer who had sold newspapers and books for more than twenty years in Halifax. He was the proprietor of a three-storey house in one of the main thoroughfares of the town – Waterhouse Street. The building held a sitting room above the shop and the floor above was Mr Crabtree's bedroom, which held a double bed that he shared with his youngest son, Samuel, aged ten. There were two more bedrooms in the building, one which held his two other sons – Walter, aged nineteen, and George, aged seventeen – and in the other slept a woman named Kate Byrne, a distant relative who was their housekeeper. Walter and George were partners in the business with their father, but it was rumoured that Walter and his father had recently argued over which direction the business should take.

At about five o'clock in the morning on Sunday, 18 December 1870, PC George Wilson was on duty and was walking past the Crabtree premises. There had been a spate of burglaries in and around the town and as he passed the shop of Crabtree & Sons he decided to check that the building was secure. As he was trying the door he heard a number of dull blows emanating from within, followed by the cry of someone in terrible distress. The policeman went to the door at the side of the house, which led into Gills Court and granted access into the building when the shop was closed. PC Wilson pounded on the door, and Walter Crabtree answered and told him that his father's throat had been cut. The constable noted that Walter was wearing only a shirt and trousers and that he had neither a waistcoat nor jacket on. The two men went upstairs where they met George, who indicated towards his father's bedroom. Inside, PC Wilson found the body of the elder William Crabtree in bed alongside his younger son, Samuel, who was very distressed. Lighting a candle they discovered that Mr Crabtree had been beaten about the head so badly that the bed was covered in blood and it was hard to recognise him. Checking for a pulse, PC Wilson found that the man was still alive but appeared to be unconscious. Walter asked, 'Who hast done this?' and Samuel replied, 'Thou knowest who has done it.' PC Wilson immediately sent Walter to the Town Hall to notify the police

'the bed was covered in blood'

that Mr Crabtree had been attacked, whilst he ran to summon the surgeon, Dr Hodgson Wright of King Cross Street. When Walter arrived at the Town Hall, he asked Sergeant Jonathon Potterton to come quickly to the house as his father had been attacked.

Kate Byrne had been woken up by the noise and, hearing what Samuel had to say, asked Walter upon his return if it was true that he had murdered his father with a poker. Walter denied it, saying he heard sounds of an attack and had gone to his father's aid. A search was made for the murder weapon and PC Wilson found a piece of wet iron in the kitchen sink. The constable took Walter's hands and noted that he had blood on the cuff of his shirt. Walter was arrested and charged with the murder of his father.

Later on, Samuel and Kate Byrne were discussing the events of that night when he mentioned that he thought the man who had attacked his father was taller than Walter. Samuel was taken to the police station the next day and was questioned about what had happened. He said that he had been sleeping next to his father when he was jolted awake by a blow to his back. He said that he could make out the outline of a man raining blows on his father's head. The candle, which had been placed on a nearby table, had been put out and as a consequence there was very little light in the bedroom. However, he was able to see that the man who attacked his father had covered his face with a piece of cloth and that he was dressed in a white shirt and dark trousers. His brother George stated that he had been woken by the sounds coming from the next room and noticed that his brother was not in the bed.

The inquest into the death of William Crabtree was held on Monday 19 December before the coroner, Mr Barstow, at the Town Hall. The crowds which attended were very large and it was decided that the inquest would simply be one of identification, so the jury went to the house to view the body. On their return the proceedings were adjourned until 3.30 p.m. later that same day. When the inquest resumed, PC Wilson described how they searched the building for the murder weapon before finding the piece of iron – which had previously been used in a printing press but now served as a poker – in the sink. The piece of metal was still wet and appeared to have been washed by the person who had committed the murder.

A post-mortem had been carried out on the day before the inquest by surgeons Mr J.H. Wright and Mr Bramley. They confirmed that Mr Crabtree's skull had been fractured in three places. On summing up, the coroner told the jury that it was apparent, given the circumstances, that the murder could only have been committed by a member of the family. The inquest had lasted for five hours and when the jury retired to deliver their verdict at 8.30 p.m. it only took five minutes for them to find Walter guilty of the wilful murder of his father. Throughout the inquest the prisoner exhibited no sense of concern or remorse, although he appeared to be upset when Samuel gave his evidence.

On Tuesday 20 December, Crabtree appeared at the Town Hall charged with his father's murder. After all the evidence had been heard Walter told the magistrate that he had been advised not to say anything. He pleaded not guilty, but the weight of evidence against him was too strong and he was committed for trial at the Leeds Assizes.

Walter Crabtree appeared at the Leeds Assizes on Wednesday, 29 March 1871 and told the court that he was not guilty. The judge, Mr Baron Cleasby, listened carefully to the evidence from the prosecution team of Mr Shaw and Mr Thornber. Crabtree appeared calm throughout most of the proceedings, but once again broke down when his

Halifax Town Hall, where Walter Crabtree reported that his father had been murdered.

younger brother gave evidence. Samuel told the court from the witness box that he shared a bed with his father and had gone to bed early, and so had no idea what time his father had retired. He broke down and cried as he described waking up to find his father being beaten over the head by a man in the bedroom. When he identified his brother as the murderer, he once more began to cry and for a short while was unable to continue with his evidence. George then took the stand and described how he had retired early, only to be woken when he felt Walter stir. Previously, he had described being woken up by Samuel's screams and rushing into his father's bedroom, where he saw Walter and had heard Samuel's accusation. Now he stated that as he awoke in the darkness he heard rustling, as if someone was getting dressed, and said, 'What's the matter?' and Walter had replied, 'I don't know.' He also stated that he had heard the noise of someone going downstairs at the same time, just after hearing the screams coming from his father's bedroom. He told the court that he had heard Samuel saying, 'Kate says it's Walter, but it wasn't Walter.' The judge asked him, 'Are you saying that Samuel kept saying that it was Walter; but it wasn't?' The witness replied, 'Yes, my Lord.'

He explained how the door on Gills Court was usually kept closed and locked, but on the night of the murder so many people had been coming in and going out that he had jammed the door open. He also explained that the same door, when it was fully opened, covered the entrance into the cellar. He said that he had heard the outer door slam when Walter and the policeman had gone to fetch the surgeon. Cross-examined by Mr Waddy, for the prosecution, he confirmed that up until the day of the murder his father and Walter had always been on good terms. He stated that, 'My father was a kind, good father to me and Walter. There was never a quarrel and I have never heard of my brother being on the liquor or misbehaving himself in any way.'

Kate Byrne told the court that she was startled awake by the sound of screaming and she immediately ran to the door of her master's bedroom, where she met Walter before he went downstairs to open the door to PC Wilson, and that in his absence she had said to Samuel that someone in the house must have murdered his father, for no one else could have done it.

The surgeon, Dr Hodgson Wright, stated that the deceased was found lying on his back on the bed and that the pillow underneath him was saturated with blood. He stated that he saw several wounds at the back of his head, which might have been caused by an instrument such as the poker, and confirmed that these wounds were the cause of death.

For the prosecution, Mr Shaw stated that the defence of the prisoner was based on the allegation that someone else had entered the house that night; he pointed out that PC George Wilson saw no one leave the house. The door from Gills Court had been locked and bolted and Sergeant Potterton had searched the house from top to bottom and found no one hiding there. Mr Shaw pointed out that the actions of the prisoner after the murder did not point to his innocence. He requested the jury take no notice of the fact that the prisoner was related to the deceased, as it did not have any bearing on their deliberations, but to treat the case as if no such relationship existed.

Mr Waddy defended his client by simply stating that, 'There was absolutely no evidence of any motive for the crime. Indeed, the prisoner had been an exemplary character and he had been on good, kind terms with his father.' He reminded them of the contradictory statement made by the youngest son and excused his confused state to being woken in such a manner. George admitted waking and hearing his brother putting on his clothes, which suggested that Walter had also heard the screams of his little brother and was dressing to investigate the matter. Mr Waddy reiterated that George had heard footsteps going down the stairs at the same time he heard his brother dressing.

The defence suggested that a burglar had secreted himself in the cellar earlier in the day with the intention of stealing what he could when the household retired. George had admitted that the door to Gills Court had been left open earlier that evening. It could have been that the burglar heard PC Wilson pounding heavily on the door to Gills Court and returned to the cellar, making his escape when they were all in the upstairs bedroom. Upon conclusion, Mr Shaw stated that there was absolutely nothing linking Walter to this crime. At the end of his speech there was considerable applause in court but this was instantly suppressed by the judge. His Lordship then proceeded to sum up the evidence and he carefully laid the two theories set up by the prosecution and the defence before the jury and called attention to the complete lack of motive for the crime. The jury retired to consider their verdict at 7.35 p.m. and ten minutes later returned back into the court. The foreman announced that they had found the prisoner not guilty.

The witness box at Leeds assizes, where ten-year-old Samuel Crabtree gave evidence against his brother.

CASE ELEVEN 1872

SAVED BY A THICK OVERCOAT

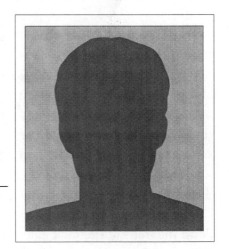

Suspect:	James Whitehead
Age:	Fifty
Charge:	Attempted Murder
Sentence:	Penal Servitude

The firm of Messrs James Akroyd & Sons Ltd of Haley Hill had long been recognised in Halifax as a worsted spinner's manufacturer, and was established by James Akroyd in 1840. As the business prospered, the family became so influential in the town that Colonel Edward Akroyd soon founded the local industrial village of Akroyden, built by architect George Gilbert Scott in 1859. This was a model village of gothic terraced houses

Akroyden, the industrial village built by Colonel E. Akroyd in 1859.

Akroyd Park, 1908.

that he built for the people he employed, and which was soon followed by another similar village built at Copley.

Colonel Akroyd lived in a mansion known as Bankfield House (now Bankfield Museum), and on his death in 1887 he left it to the people of Halifax for a nominal cost of £6,000. The house and surrounding parkland became known as Akroyd Park, in memory of its benefactor, and is a popular location with the people of Halifax today.

The company of Akroyd & Sons Ltd employed about 4,000 employees in the different departments at their works on Haley Hill, and such was its esteem that the factory was visited by the future Edward VII after he had officially opened the Town Hall in Halifax in 1863. In 1872, the firm was flourishing and it was Colonel Akroyd who appointed his wife's nephew, Mr John Edward Champney, as a partner in the company. Mr Champney played an active role in the firm, as well as being a local magistrate who lived at Northowram.

On Friday, 15 November 1872, Mr Champney left the house at Bankfield, where he usually had lunch with his aunt and uncle. As he was going through the gates of the works he saw James Whitehead on the opposite side of the road. Whitehead, aged fifty, had been employed as a supervisor at the Haley Hill mill for many years but had been dismissed for drunken behaviour the previous year. After being out of work for some time he had approached Mr Champney to ask for his job back and been re-instated as a loom weaver. However, it was not long before his reliability was again compromised when, on 24 October 1872, he refused to follow instructions and he was once more dismissed.

In November 1872, Mr Champney was on holiday with his family and the mill was being run by another manager, who found it necessary to dismiss another man working at the mill named John Gray – Whitehead's brother-in-law. It had been announced that Gray was under investigation and as a result, and in order to escape the inquiries, Gray was allowed to hand in his notice. After his dismissal, Gray died, although no reason was given for his demise. Whatever the cause, Whitehead attached the blame for both his and his relative's dismissal on Mr Champney and began to plot his revenge.

So when Mr Champney saw Whitehead on the afternoon of 15 November, he wished to avoid him and continued to walk down Haley Hill, not knowing that Whitehead was following him. Champney called in at the schoolroom attached to the works and when he emerged at 3.30 p.m. he saw Whitehead once again. Champney then went into the works' weaving shed, where

Bankfield House, now Bankfield Museum.

700 people were employed, and continued to conduct business until 5 p.m. He spoke to one of the supervisors and told him that if Whitehead wanted some work to employ him again on one of the looms. When he came out of the works he walked towards Cross Hill. After walking for only a short distance he heard a shot behind him and felt a heavy blow behind his left shoulder blade. When he looked back he saw Whitehead about three yards away holding a pistol, and as he turned he felt another blow on his back. In anger, Champney turned and struck out at Whitehead, hitting him on the side of his head with his umbrella, the handle of which broke from the force of the blow. Fearing

'he heard a shot behind him'

that Whitehead was once more going to shoot him, Champney quickly made his way back to the office of the works, where he saw Mr Stansfield and told him that he had been fired at. Mr Bramley, a surgeon, was sent for and, upon examining Champney, found two bullets – which had been fashioned out of a piece of iron from a weaving rod – trapped between his braces and his waistcoat. As he removed his outer coat and inner jacket the first bullet fell to the floor. The second bullet, which had just penetrated the skin, was removed by Mr Bramley, before he dressed Champney's wounds. Whitehead was quickly arrested and taken to the Town Hall.

A typical weaving mill in Halifax similar to the one owned by Messrs J. Akroyd & Sons on Haley Hill where James Whitehead had been employed.

The following day, Whitehead was brought into the Halifax Borough Court and charged with the shooting and attempted murder of Mr Champney. The prisoner was asked how he pleaded, to which he stated that he was not guilty. The Chief Constable, Mr Clarkson, outlined the case before the magistrate, who ordered that Whitehead was to be remanded until Tuesday 19 November.

While in court, Champney told of Whitehead's dismissal, feeling the bullets on his back and how he had struck the prisoner over the head. Another witness, a man named Thomas Best, stated that Whitehead had been seen near the door of the weaving shed between 3 p.m. and 4 p.m., and that he had noticed that the prisoner seemed a bit worse for wear. He had spoken to Whitehead and asked him what he was up to, to which Whitehead replied he was there to kill Champney. Another witness, Thomas Parker, stated that he was coming home from the mill at 5.10 p.m. Just as he was passing the Coach and Horse Inn on Haley Hill he spotted Whitehead standing near to Mr Champney, just before the latter hit him over the head with his umbrella. Sergeant Turner took the stand next and described how he had arrested Whitehead. He could see that he had been drinking and after charging him, asked him if he fully understood what he was being charged with. Whitehead told him that he did and that it was alright.

The magistrates consulted with each other before summing up the case for the jury. They took only a short time for deliberation before Whitehead was found guilty and committed to take his trial at the next assizes.

On Friday, 6 December 1872, Whitehead was brought before the Leeds Assizes. He was undefended, and the prosecution was undertaken by Mr Waddy and Mr Wavell. Mr Waddy told the court that the prosecution had been promoted by the directors of the company of J. Akroyd & Son Ltd on a charge of attempted murder. He also told the jury that there could be no doubt about the premeditation of the action taken by the prisoner. Mr Waddy stated that when charged with the offence, Whitehead had again confirmed this statement in a cell at the Halifax police station. The home-made bullet was then produced for the court and it still had a portion of the cloth from the victim's overcoat attached to it. Mr Waddy categorically stated that only the thickness of the overcoat had stopped the wounds from being more serious. The coat was shown to the court and both bullet holes were clearly visible. In his defence, Whitehead asked Mr Champney if he was certain that it had been himself who had fired the gun that evening, as it had been quite dark and that the street light had been behind him, but Mr Champney stated with absolute certainty that it was Whitehead who had fired the pistol.

Next to take the stand was Thomas Best, who, when asked if Whitehead had been sober when he spoke to him, told the court that Whitehead had been very drunk but seemed determined to carry out his intentions. He was then asked why he hadn't alerted Mr Champney to the threat and he replied that he thought Whitehead was too drunk to carry it out. The other witness, Thomas Parker, also gave his account, stating that Whitehead had been waiting for Mr Champney. He had advised him to come back in the morning but Whitehead had just shaken his head.

Inspector John Helliwell Thompson of the Halifax police stated that a member of the Watch Committee, Mr Kershaw, had talked to Whitehead in his cell on the day after his arrest. He told Whitehead that he was sorry to see him there and asked why he had done it and he told him that, 'He had sacked John Gray and he sacked me.' The surgeon gave evidence regarding the wounds he had found on Mr Champney and said that had the bullets penetrated a quarter of an inch deeper the results would have been fatal. Whitehead was asked if he wished to ask any of the witnesses any questions, but he declined. The judge summed up for the jury, who returned a verdict of guilty. The judge then told the prisoner:

> You appear to be a very desperate man and the only way of accounting for your actions was that you had been drinking. As such, I can only conclude that you had lost your reason and all that lifts a man to be something higher than a mere brute. Now you have reduced yourself to the condition of having shot at a fellow creature with the intent to kill him; and it was only providential circumstances that saved the intended victim's life.

Offering no clemency or mercy to the prisoner, he ordered that he be sentenced to fifteen years penal servitude.

CASE TWELVE 1889

'ACTING LIKE JACK THE RIPPER'

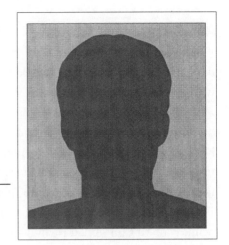

Suspect: Frederick Brett
Age: Forty-two
Charge: Murder
Sentence: Executed

In October 1889, the Jack the Ripper murders were still being widely talked about throughout England. There is little doubt that the story of the gruesome murders affected many people who read them. One was a man called Frederick Brett, from Halifax, who attributed the murder of his wife to the impact that Jack the Ripper had on him.

It seems that Frederick Brett, aged forty-two, and his wife Margaret, aged thirty-eight, had gone to Halifax in the latter part of July 1889 to work on the Halifax High Level Railway. The life of railway navvies and their wives were difficult, and many had to live in huts and sheds erected near to the place where they would be working. Brett was slightly luckier than some of his comrades because he had been in the Army Reserve Corp and had received a small pension. Within a matter of weeks he had given up the life of a navvy, due to allegations that his wife was too free with other men, and had obtained another position working at a brickyard at Elland. The couple had also managed to get lodgings at Gibbet Street, Halifax, in the home of Mr James Hindley.

Sunday, 20 October 1889, started as a normal day for Margaret and Frederick. Relations between the couple had steadily been getting worse, as Frederick's increasing bouts of jealousy resulted in rows and arguments. According to their landlord, they had returned from the pub about 11.30 p.m. the night before and Brett had said to his wife, 'Maggie, you seem to treat me so lightly, if you don't want me, say so and let me go at once.' She told him to shut up and the next thing he heard was the couple going upstairs to bed.

Despite the fact that they had only been married a couple of years, Margaret and Frederick's days started, all too frequently, with a row, resulting in the pair being incredibly sulky and barely speaking to one another over breakfast, and this Sunday was no different. However, by noon Brett had agreed to go to the pub to fetch a quart of beer for them to share with their lunch. After lunch he asked Margaret to go to the pub again for two more quarts of beer. At first she refused but, finally, to placate him she went, although when she returned she refused to drink any of it. By about 3 p.m., Brett had finished off all the beer and his wife decided to go out, but he wouldn't let her go and in a temper he pushed her towards the bottom of the stairs, telling her to go to the bedroom and that he would follow her up. A few minutes later, the landlord heard screams and Margaret crying out. On reaching the bedroom, he found Margaret on the bed with blood pouring from a wound in her throat and Brett on top of her with an open pocket knife in his hand. Hindley recognised the knife as his own and pulled at Brett to try to get him off his wife. Brett stood up with the bloodstained knife in his hand and turned towards Hindley. The old man backed away, missed his footing and fell down the stairs. After making his way to the front door, Hindley raised the alarm before going to find a policeman.

'The old man backed away, missed his footing and fell down the stairs'

Meanwhile, Brett calmly sat in the kitchen and lit a clay pipe and began to smoke it. After hearing the commotion, some of the neighbours had arrived on the scene, and one of them asked him why he had done it. He illogically told them, 'What's done can't be undone, but she was a good lass to me.' In response to a similar question from another neighbour, he answered, 'I have only been acting like Jack the Ripper.' He then made a move to leave but the neighbours held on to him until the police arrived.

Mr Henry Smith, a surgeon of Rhodes Street, was sent for but Margaret was dead before he arrived. Brett, meanwhile, was taken to the Town Hall and questioned before being arrested on a charge of murder.

The same night an inquest was held into the death of Margaret Brett at the Granby Inn in front of the coroner, Mr Barstow. Before the inquest began the jury viewed the body as it lay in the coffin. The first witness to be heard was the surgeon, Mr Smith, who told the jury that the wound in the woman's throat had severed the major vessels and that it could not have been self-inflicted. He stated that, judging by the serious nature of her injuries, death must have been almost instantaneous.

James Hindley then described the day's events and his horror at seeing the woman on the bed, her throat covered in blood. He told the coroner that relations had been so bad between the couple that he had asked them to leave the premises on several occasions. Another neighbour, John Denton, corroborated Hindley's evidence and stated that after the old man had raised the alarm he had gone into the house and seen the woman's body on the bed. Police constable Turner gave evidence next, saying that he had been on duty in Gibbet Street when Hindley had approached him and told him that a murder had been com-

'death must have been almost instantaneous'

mitted at his house. He immediately went to the address, but when he got there the woman was already dead. He asked Brett where the knife was but he replied that he did not know. The knife was later given up to

Gibbet Street, Halifax, where Frederick Brett and his wife Margaret found lodgings.

PC Turner, who showed it to Brett and asked him if that was the knife he had used to cut his wife's throat, and Brett agreed that it was. When asked by the coroner if Brett had anything to say in his own defence, he replied, 'No Sir.' After a very brief consultation, the jury returned a verdict of wilful murder.

On Monday 21 October at noon, Brett was brought before the Halifax Borough Court where the magistrate, Mr E.M. Wavell, heard the case. Brett gave his name and address and told the court that he had lived at Manchester until a few weeks previously, when he had moved to Halifax. He stated that during their brief married life his wife had scandalized him and that he could do nothing right for her. The Chief Constable, Mr Pole, stated that the prisoner knew no one in Halifax and, because he was virtually unknown, he needed to make further enquiries about him from Manchester and requested a remand for the prisoner to the following day. The remand was granted and the inquiry was adjourned. When the inquiry resumed, little material evidence was heard and it seems that Brett had previously been of good character, although it was said that he was addicted to drink. The magistrate summed up the evidence and found him guilty of the wilful murder of his wife and committed him to stand trial at the next assizes.

'found him guilty of the wilful murder of his wife'

Brett appeared at the winter assizes in Leeds on Friday, 13 December 1889, in front of Mr Justice Manisty. He was defended by Mr C. Mellor, and Mr C. Briscoe and Mr Harold Thomas acted for the prosecution. Mr Thomas opened the case by stating that when the couple had initially moved to Halifax, they had seemed amicable enough for the first fortnight, but then they started rowing. Mr Hindley was not happy about the way that Brett spoke to his wife and had complained about it on several occasions. Brett, in return, complained to him that his wife was too free with the other navvies. The prosecution agreed and stated that the motive for the murder was jealousy of his wife's conduct with other men. His defence stated that at

Armley Gaol, where Frederick Brett spent his last few days before execution.

the time of the crime, Brett had been sodden with drink and did not know what he was doing, but the judge countered that it was all too common an excuse and therefore it could not been seen as an argument for his defence. The judge summed up in minute detail all the points which the jury needed to consider, and they took just over an hour to find him guilty. Mr Justice Manisty put on the black cap and, in very solemn tones, sentenced Brett to death.

On Tuesday, 31 December 1889, Brett was hanged at Leeds Armley Gaol. As the clock struck 8 a.m. Brett walked boldly towards the scaffold and, after making sure the hood was put on and the noose arranged around his head, the bolt was

It was through this building at Armley Gaol where the executed bodies of prisoners were removed for burial on a site which is now a car park for the staff of the prison.

drawn and he was launched into eternity. The black flag was hoisted at the prison gate to let the people assembled know that the execution had taken place.

CASE THIRTEEN   1892

MURDER IN THE CELLAR

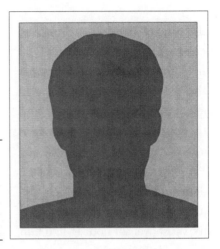

Suspect:	Arthur Shaw
Age:	Seventeen
Charge:	Murder
Sentence:	Penal Servitude

On Thursday, 24 May 1892, at Calder Street, Caddyfield, sixty-six-year-old widow Mrs Susan Townsend was found battered in her home, lying almost insensible. Discovered by her neighbour, Mrs Adeline Shaw, she appeared to be seriously injured; her face covered with blood. A bloodstained hammer was found near the door of the cellar. The doctor was called for and she was taken to Halifax Infirmary, where a nurse heard her cry out, 'Oh don't hit me again with that hammer!' She later told one of the nurses that a man had hit her. Mrs Townsend died from her injuries at about 6 a.m on Monday 30 May.

Halifax Infirmary, where Mrs Susan Townsend spent her last hours on 24 May 1892.

It seems that the police were suspicious of seventeen-year-old Arthur Shaw, the son of Adeline Shaw, who told the police that she and her husband would not allow their son to live with them due to his bad character. The police made a number of investigations into the crime and questioned Arthur Shaw, but little could be proved and they were forced to let him go.

'her face covered with blood'

The inquest was held before the coroner, Mr Barstow, on 1 June 1892 at the mortuary on Lister Lane. The jury viewed the body at the Infirmary and listened to the evidence of some of the nurses, as well as one of the other patients, a woman named Ester Simpson, who had known the victim before her untimely demise. She stated that when asked whether a man had attacked her, Townsend had replied, 'No.' She then asked if a woman had done it, and again she replied, 'No.' The nurses stated that their patient was clearly confused, no doubt due to the terrible injuries she had received. Simpson revealed to the jury that the deceased woman had previously considered taking her own life. She stated that about six weeks previously, Mrs Townsend had told her that she had been up all night and if she could have found a piece of rope she would have hung herself because she was tired of living.

The jury returned to the mortuary and the inquest was reconvened in the presence of the Chief Constable of Halifax, Mr Pole. Dr Adams, the house

Lister Lane, Halifax, as it is today.

surgeon at the Infirmary, stated that Mrs Townsend had four serious scalp wounds and it was more than likely the skull had been fractured in four places. He expressed the opinion that the wounds could not possibly have been self-inflicted, nor could they have happened from a fall. Despite the hammer, which was found in the basement with blood and hair attached to it, the jury deliberated and returned an open verdict, claiming that there was no evidence to show how the wounds had been inflicted.

At the end of January 1893, Arthur Shaw, now a prisoner in Wakefield Gaol, confessed to the crime, stating that it had been on his mind and he could not rest. He was serving a two-month prison sentence for a gross assault on a little girl at Ovenden and during his incarceration he had tried to commit suicide twice. He had asked to speak to the governor of Wakefield Gaol and confessed to killing Mrs Townsend. The governor then communicated with the Chief Constable of Halifax, who went to see him at Wakefield on 10 February, along with the deputy magistrate's clerk, who took the confession down in writing. Shaw admitted that he had been living at a lodging house on Winding Road, Halifax, and had gone to his mother's house at about 10 p.m. to borrow a penny to pay for his lodgings. When his mother told him that she had no money, Shaw then went to Mrs Townsend's house to see if he could borrow the money from her. As he approached the house he saw Sarah Butterworth leaving, but she didn't see him as he claimed that she was drunk. He entered Mrs Townsend's house and he said that she also appeared to be a little drunk.

As he entered, the old lady was sitting in a chair near the fireplace with her back to him and a shawl over her shoulders. He asked her if his mother could borrow her coal hammer and she replied, 'Yes lad, get it, it's in the coal cellar.' He asked her for a penny, but she told him that she had spent her last penny on beer. Shaw described how he waited a long time, swinging the hammer about, unsure whether to strike her or not. He had heard that she had money in the house and with this in mind he struck her once, and she fell forward in her chair. He searched the house and found nothing, and then, because he knew that she would be able to identify him, he hit her three more times on the back of her head. He then calmly went back to his lodging house, only once being stopped by a constable at Caddyfield Bridge, who asked him what he was doing out so late at night. When he told him he was going to

Winding Road, Halifax, where Arthur Shaw had lodgings.

his lodgings, the constable told him that he should have been at his lodgings earlier and advised him to get off home.

In the morning, he had returned to his mother's house, who told him about finding her neighbour badly injured. She also told him that the police wanted to see him at the Town Hall. Mr Pole interviewed him and asked him if he seen any suspicious people when he had left his mother's house the previous night and he answered that he had seen some workmen, who looked like they had finished work and were on their way home. Shaw told him that he had been at his lodging house all night and the Chief Constable, unable to find any evidence against him, allowed him to go home. However, the matter had preyed on Shaw's mind and he had decided to confess.

After listening to his statement, Chief Constable Pole asked him to sign the written version, but before he did so, Shaw added another couple of sentences. He stated that he had gone to the old woman's house with the intention of killing her and stealing her money and to stay at her house for the night before travelling to Hull the next day. He then signed the confession, adding at the bottom: 'I make this statement entirely of my own free will and because the matter is continually troubling my mind as I cannot think of anything else.' Once he had signed the statement, the Chief Constable asked him if he had anything else to say, to which he replied he did not.

On Friday 3 March, Shaw was taken from Wakefield Gaol to Halifax Borough Court, where he pleaded guilty to the charge of wilful murder. He was closely attended by one of the warders – a man named Stephenson. Mr Keighley Walton, for the prosecution, opened the case and the Chief

Constable read out Shaw's confession. After hearing all the evidence the jury returned a verdict of guilty of wilful murder, and Shaw was sent to stand trial at the next assizes.

On Thursday 16 March, Shaw appeared at the Leeds Assizes, where he pleaded guilty to murder. He had no defence and no evidence was offered on his behalf. He appeared to be calm when coming up from the cells into the courtroom. After it was discovered that he had been given the nickname 'Mad Shaw' while he had been working as a ship's cook, an enquiry into the state of his mental health was carried out. As a result of this, the judge ordered that Dr Henry Clarke, the medical officer at Wakefield Gaol, attend the assizes and give his opinion of whether Shaw was fit to plead; the assizes were adjourned until later that day. During the short hearing, Shaw gave the impression of being quite unaware of the seriousness of his crime as he gazed around him at the other people in the court. Later, when the trial was reconvened, Dr Clarke said that he had observed the prisoner since he was first brought to Wakefield Gaol and offered the opinion that he was perfectly competent to plead. It took a matter of five minutes after Shaw's appearance in the dock for the judge, Justice Bruce, to read out the death sentence. Shaw showed no reaction to the sentence, but it caused a great sensation in the crowded court.

Despite Dr Clarke's assurances that Shaw was fit to plead, doubts were expressed about his sanity. Another medical man, Dr Lewis from the Wakefield Asylum, was asked to assess Shaw and give his opinion. He stated that Shaw was insane and therefore incapable of understanding his crime. The judge was criticized for sentencing Shaw to death, despite the fact that he had sought a medical opinion before sentencing him. Following Dr Lewis's opinion, attempts were then made by the people of Halifax to have the death sentence commuted to life imprisonment. On Monday 27 March it was announced that a petition was being collected in Halifax in favour of his reprieve. The petition was passed to the Home Secretary in London later that week, with almost 2,000 signatures on it – many from the most respectable industrialists of the town. In the meantime, Shaw had written a letter to his mother which read:

> I am quite happy and contented, but have a hope I get pardoned by the Home Secretary. You know while there is life, there is hope. I am paying strict attention to the chaplain's advice and I have felt a lot happier since

you can come and see me any day. But you must not walk it. If you cannot get the money, write instead. I might get pardoned yet. You can write to the Home Secretary, Home Office London and plead for me. It will do a lot of good. Ask him to have mercy on me as I am only very young. You must state my case to him, and you might be able to save me. Do not forget it is my only hope. You know I have not written up myself, but I will do so and I hope if I do get pardoned that you will always write to me. Will you please write by return and let me know if you have written to the Home Office; it will cheer me up more still. Dear mother, I am prepared for the worst if it comes. I am quite safe, I am sure, and if we never meet on earth, I hope to meet in heaven. What made me do it, God only knows. But if I do get off, I shall still keep the chaplains words.

His mother went to Armley Gaol to visit her son, and afterwards told reporters that she was surprised to see him looking so well. He had seemed more hopeful when she told him that she was going to contact the Home Secretary, but she told him not to get his hopes up for a response. She wrote to the Home Secretary stating that the evidence of Dr Lewis had said that her son was of unsound mind and that she felt, as a mother, he was not answerable for this dreadful charge. It was finally announced on Tuesday 28 March that a reprieve had been given by the Home Secretary and that Shaw's sentence had been commuted to penal servitude for life.

This case underlines the ambiguity that some judges had towards people with mental health issues throughout the Victorian era. The McNaghten Rule, which was made in 1843 following the attempted assassination of the Prime Minister, Robert Peel, became a standard test in establishing criminal responsibility in cases of insanity. Nevertheless, cases which had to prove whether or not the prisoner was insane meant that judges and magistrates still had to rely on medical opinion, which, as we have seen, could be in opposition. In such cases the prisoner was usually kept in an asylum at Her Majesty's pleasure and the death sentence could not be imposed upon them.

MURDER AND SUICIDE

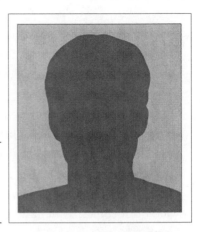

Suspect:	Ephraim Smith
Age:	About forty
Charge:	Murder/Suicide

Carpet manufacturing was a common trade throughout Halifax, and one company in particular became world famous; Crossley Carpets. The works were started by John Crossley in around 1822 at Crossley Mill, where he employed a workforce of around 300 people. Rapid expansion led to more factories being built on the site, which now spreads out over

Crossley's original mill, which was built around 1822.

North Bridge, Halifax, 1906.

20 acres and can be seen behind North Bridge. The site is now known as the Dean Clough works and has around 150 businesses within its walls.

A man named Ephraim Smith, around forty-years-old, was employed as a carpet weaver at the works and was known to be a good, steady, reliable worker. Smith was caring for his three children, William, aged thirteen, Elizabeth, aged ten and Emma, aged five, at their home, which was one small room at the top of a three-storey building on Lee Bank. Despite his regular employment the house was described as being wretchedly furnished and, as was usual in those times, the occupants all slept in the same bed. The children's mother had been removed to the Wakefield Lunatic Asylum two years previously and it was known that the loss of his wife had left Smith very low-spirited at times.

On Saturday, 30 June 1866, William had gone to a fair in Halifax and returned home later than usual at about 11 p.m. He was surprised to find the house in darkness and the door locked and bolted. He called out to his father to let him in but there was no response. He managed to open a window close to the door and put his arm through to let himself into the house. Once inside, he struck a match and was horrified to find Elizabeth at the back of the door and his father lying a few yards away from her, both with their throats cut. He ran to the nearest house to raise the alarm and two neighbours, a man named Solomon Broadbent, and a retired policeman, Gibson Walton, followed the boy back into the house. Blood was splattered all over the floor and walls as well as over a mirror which was hanging on the wall. Ephriam Smith's body was leaning against a wall underneath the front window. The cut in his throat was so deep that it had almost severed his head from his shoulders. All around him was a large pool of blood and an open razor was found on the floor, about half a yard away from his body. Behind the door was the body of Elizabeth, also lying in a pool of blood. It was evident that she had struggled with her attacker, as her hands were covered in slash marks.

The two men went upstairs where they found the body of the youngest child, Emma, also dead; she had been suffocated. It was thought that she had been held face downwards on the bed and smothered with the bed-clothes. A constable was sent for and when he spoke to the neighbours it appears that only one neighbour had heard any noise at all, and that had been at around ten o'clock. After investigating the scene of the crime, it was

Lee Bank, where Ephraim Smith lived with his three children in 1866.

deduced that Ephraim had committed the crime; killing the younger child first, then Elizabeth, before he committed suicide.

'The cut in his throat was so deep that it had almost severed his head from his shoulders'

The inquest was held before the coroner, Mr Dyson, on Monday, 2 July 1866 at the Shears Inn, Lee Bridge. The first witness called was William Greenwood, a carpet weaver who had worked with Smith for about ten years. Although he told the coroner that Smith's conduct had been rather strange at times, he had never heard him complain about his children or treat them unkindly, nor had he said anything about killing himself or the children and had shown no sign of it in his behaviour. Greenwood admitted that since his wife had been taken away, Smith had been low-spirited at times but stated that despite his depression, he was a hard-working, quiet, diligent man.

William Smith stated that his father had not been drinking during the week of the murder and neither was he given to be drunk. He told the inquest that his father had been behaving rather strangely the week before the murders and that he had tried to commit suicide once before, after his mother had been taken to Wakefield. He then described entering the house and finding the bodies.

Solomon Broadbent, Smith's neighbour, told the inquest that they had been a quiet family and he had noticed nothing strange in his neighbour's behaviour. He said that Smith had always appeared to be good and kind with his children. Another neighbour, Grace Wade, also agreed with the previous witness and said that the family was quiet and retiring in their nature. She said that although they had all been very distressed when their mother had been taken to the lunatic asylum, matters seemed to have improved for them of late. Wade had gone to the house after hearing the alarm and she described how several articles of furniture had blood smeared on them, and that Emma's face had been pushed deep into the bedding.

PC Wilson said that he had heard of the murders and went to the house at 11.20 p.m., which, by now, was full of people. He then described finding the razor, before he produced it for the coroner; it was noted that it was still smeared with blood. William Smith identified the razor as belonging to his father. Mr J. Hodgson Wright, the surgeon, described the bodies, which he had examined just before 1 a.m. on the Sunday morning. He said that Smith's wound was quite deep, about four inches long across the neck, and so severe that death would have been immediate. The older girl had a wound about the same size and depth, along with a slight wound on the right-hand thumb and left knuckles. She also had slight bruising to her hands and arms. He said that the youngest child had been suffocated and that she too had bruises on her arms as if she had struggled with her father.

Gibson Walton stated that he had heard nothing untoward coming from the house on the night, but had noticed that Smith had sent Elizabeth running on several errands for him. The coroner supposed that during this time Smith had killed the youngest child. In summing up, the coroner stated that he thought that Smith had deliberately planned the murders and that he would have killed his son as well if he had been at home. Fortunately he had been late coming home from the fair, a fact which had saved his life. The jury returned a verdict of guilty of murder, but what state of mind he was in at the time could not be ascertained. There was little doubt that Smith had been a steady and industrious man and his general conduct in the neighbourhood was such that people found it hard to believe that he had committed this heinous crime.

Lightning Source UK Ltd.
Milton Keynes UK
UKOW031710240413

209707UK00002B/6/P